Canon EOS R6 Mark II
User Guide

Master Every Button, Autofocus Mode, and Video Setting with

Step-by-Step Tutorials, Digital Photography Tricks, and Real-Life

Shooting Scenarios for Beginners, Seniors, and Content Creators

Randy Osborn

Copyright © 2025 by Randy Osborn

recommendations presented. The use of any camera gear or shooting method is solely at the reader's discretion and risk.

Always consult the official Canon user manual or authorized Canon support for up-to-date product specifications, firmware changes, and warranty-related concerns.

By reading this book, you acknowledge that the author and publisher shall not be held liable for any loss, damage, or injury resulting from the use or misuse of the information provided.

How to Use This Book

Whether you are just unboxing your Canon EOS R6 Mark II for the first time or you've already been shooting with it for a while, this book is designed to help you get results quickly without feeling overwhelmed.

Here's how to navigate it based on your needs:

- **Beginners** – Start with *Part I: Getting Started*. It walks you through your camera's layout, basic setup, and core functions, so you can begin taking great photos without sifting through every page of the official manual.

- **Seniors** – Throughout the book, look for tips on simplifying menus, customizing buttons, and using the camera's touchscreen features to make shooting easier and more enjoyable.

- **Content Creators & Hybrid Shooters** – Head straight to *Part III: Cinematography & Video Mastery*. It's packed with guidance on 4K/6K video, cinematic frame rates, color grading, and stabilizing your footage for professional results.

Practical Flow of the Book:

- *Part I* helps you set up and feel comfortable with your camera.

- *Part II* dives into still photography techniques and real-world scenarios.

- *Part III* focuses entirely on video and cinematography, covering everything from frame rates to editing workflows.

- *Part IV* expands your skills with lens recommendations, post-processing tips, and creative challenges.

- *Part V* gives you quick-reference cheat sheets and troubleshooting advice for when things don't go as planned.

By the time you finish, you'll not only know what every button does, but also how to use those functions creatively to tell better stories — whether in a single still image or a cinematic video sequence.

Table of Contents

Preface

Master your Canon EOS R6 Mark II and unlock its full creative potential with this complete Canon EOS R6 Mark II User Guide — the Canon R6 Mark II Manual designed for real-world photographers and filmmakers. Whether you're searching for the perfect Canon R6 Mark II for Beginners or an advanced Canon R6 Mark II for Seniors resource, this all-in-one Canon R6 Mark II Photography Guide and Canon R6 Mark II Video Guide delivers everything you need. From Canon R6 Mark II Setup Instructions to expert Canon R6 Mark II Autofocus Settings and Canon R6 Mark II 4K Video Settings, you'll get a true Canon R6 Mark II Cinematography Guide that empowers you to shoot like a pro.

Inside this Canon R6 Mark II Camera Book and Canon Mirrorless Camera Guide, you'll learn how to use Canon EOS R6 Mark II confidently, mastering everything from Canon R6 Mark II Color Profiles to Canon R6 Mark II Wedding Photography, Canon R6 Mark II Sports Photography, Canon R6 Mark II Landscape

Photography, and Canon R6 Mark II Portrait Photography. Discover Canon R6 Mark II Manual Controls, Learn Canon EOS R6 Mark II Fast with Easy Photography Tutorials for Canon EOS R6 Mark II, and Master Manual Mode Canon R6 Mark II without the overwhelm.

You'll follow Step-by-Step Camera Settings Canon R6 Mark II and apply Real-Life Camera Shooting Recipes in a Beginner-Friendly Canon R6 Mark II Guide trusted by enthusiasts and pros alike. Recognized as the Best Canon R6 Mark II Book for Filmmakers, this guide is packed with Canon R6 Mark II Tips and Tricks to Unlock Canon R6 Mark II Potential and Improve Your Photography with Canon R6 Mark II.

Get the Best Canon R6 Mark II Settings for Portraits, learn How to Film in 4K with Canon R6 Mark II, and achieve cinematic shots with Cinematic Video Settings Canon EOS R6 Mark II. Explore Canon R6 Mark II Eye Tracking Autofocus Guide, techniques for Shooting in Low Light with Canon EOS R6 Mark II, and a Complete

Guide to Canon R6 Mark II for Beginners that explains Canon R6 Mark II Manual Mode Explained in plain language.

For filmmakers, discover How to Use C-Log 3 on Canon EOS R6 Mark II, professional Canon R6 Mark II Wedding Videography Settings, and Canon R6 Mark II Sports and Action Shooting Tips. Whether you're following a mirrorless photography guide beginners path or experimenting with cinematic video canon r6 mark ii, this book shows exactly how to shoot in manual mode canon, fine-tune canon r6 mark ii autofocus tips tricks, set beginner canon video recording settings, and apply the best settings canon r6 mark ii portraits. Sports lovers will also enjoy sports action photography canon mirrorless insights for capturing fast-moving subjects with stunning clarity.

This isn't just a manual — it's your constant field companion for turning inspiration into breathtaking stills and videos.

Introduction

The Canon EOS R6 Mark II isn't just another camera in the lineup — it's a creative powerhouse designed for those who refuse to compromise on quality, whether behind the lens or in front of the timeline in post-production. From still photographers chasing the perfect moment to filmmakers crafting cinematic narratives, the R6 Mark II bridges worlds with precision, speed, and stunning image fidelity.

Yet, for all its brilliance, this camera can be overwhelming when you first take it out of the box. Buttons and dials seem endless, menus run deep, and the technical terms — ISO, bitrate, IBIS, C-Log 3 — can leave even seasoned shooters flipping through the official manual and searching online for plain-English explanations.

That's where this book comes in. This is your independent, hands-on guide to mastering the Canon EOS R6 Mark II without the trial-and-error guesswork. You won't find recycled spec sheets or dry, one-line definitions here. Instead, you'll get field-tested tips, real-life shooting scenarios, and clear, step-by-step instructions crafted for beginners, seniors, hobbyists, and working content creators alike.

Across these pages, we'll strip away jargon and walk through every essential — from the basics of setting up your camera, to unlocking its most advanced autofocus capabilities, to making the leap into professional-grade cinematography. You'll learn how to adapt the R6 Mark II for portraits, sports, landscapes, weddings, documentaries, and even short films. You'll discover how to capture rich, cinematic video with the right frame rates, color profiles, and stabilization techniques. And you'll explore editing workflows that preserve your creative vision from the moment you press the shutter to the moment you share your final masterpiece.

This isn't about memorizing settings — it's about understanding them. Once you know why your camera behaves the way it does in different conditions, you'll move past the fear of missing a shot and into the confidence of creating exactly what you envision.

Whether you're picking up the R6 Mark II as your first serious camera or upgrading from another system, this book is your bridge from curiosity to mastery. The goal is simple: when you finish reading, you'll not only know how to use your Canon EOS R6 Mark II — you'll know how to make it an extension of your own eye, your own hands, and your own creative voice.

Let's begin. The world is full of moments worth capturing — and your R6 Mark II is ready.

Part I: Getting Started

Chapter 1

Unboxing & First Impressions

There's a quiet kind of excitement that comes with opening the box of a brand-new camera. The smell of fresh packaging, the feel of untouched buttons, the weight of the gear in your hands — it's more than just a transaction; it's the beginning of a relationship with a tool that will help you capture countless moments. The Canon EOS R6 Mark II isn't just another camera body. It's the start of a creative journey that blends technology, artistry, and your own unique vision.

What's in the Box

When you first open the packaging, take a moment to appreciate how Canon has neatly organized everything. You'll typically find the following items:

- **Canon EOS R6 Mark II Camera Body** – carefully wrapped, with a protective body cap over the lens mount to shield the sensor from dust.

- **Camera Strap** – branded, adjustable, and designed to distribute weight comfortably across your shoulder or neck.

- **Battery Pack (LP-E6NH)** – Canon's robust rechargeable battery, capable of extended shooting sessions.

- **Battery Charger** – compact and lightweight, with clear indicators for charging status.

- **USB Interface Cable** – for data transfer or charging if your model supports it.

- **Official Canon Documentation** – warranty card, quick start guide, and safety instructions.

If you purchased a kit rather than the body alone, you might also find a Canon RF lens, lens caps, and a soft protective pouch. Always double-check against your purchase list to ensure nothing is missing before you discard the packaging.

First Checks Before You Shoot

It's tempting to attach a lens, flick the power switch, and start firing off shots immediately. But a few smart checks will ensure your camera is ready for trouble-free shooting.

1. **Charge the Battery Fully**

   Remove the LP-E6NH battery from its packaging and place it in the charger. A solid orange light means it's charging; a green light means it's ready. Even if the battery comes partially charged, top it up fully — lithium-ion batteries benefit from complete charges before first use.

2. **Insert a Compatible Memory Card**

   The R6 Mark II supports high-speed SD UHS-II cards, which are ideal for 4K video and burst photography. Insert the card into the correct slot with the label facing the back of the camera. Push gently until it clicks into place.

3. **Perform a Firmware Check**

   Firmware is the camera's internal operating system, and

Canon occasionally releases updates to improve performance, add features, or fix bugs. Navigate to the setup menu, scroll to "Firmware," and check the version number. If an update is available from Canon's website, download it onto your SD card and follow the on-screen update prompts.

4. **Attach a Lens (If Available)**

Remove the body cap from the camera and the rear cap from your lens. Align the mounting marks — a red dot for RF lenses — and gently twist until it locks with a satisfying click. Never force the lens; it should mount smoothly.

Setting Up the Strap

A camera strap might seem like a minor accessory, but it's your first line of defense against accidental drops. Threading it correctly also prevents the strap from loosening over time.

- Pass the strap's narrow end through the camera's lug from underneath.

- Thread it through the plastic fastener, loop it back through the strap adjuster, and pull it snug.

- Repeat on the other side, making sure the strap lies flat without twists.

For heavier lenses or long shooting days, consider investing in a padded cross-body sling strap, which distributes weight more evenly.

Protecting Your Camera from Day One

A few simple steps now can save you from expensive repairs later:

- **Use a UV or clear protective filter** on your lens to guard against scratches and dust.

- **Keep the body cap on** whenever a lens isn't attached.

- **Avoid touching the sensor** — cleaning it requires specialized tools or professional service.

- **Store the camera in a padded bag** when not in use, especially during travel.

- **Invest in a rain cover or weather protection sleeve** if you plan to shoot outdoors in unpredictable conditions.

The first time you hold the Canon EOS R6 Mark II, you'll notice its reassuring weight and solid grip. It feels balanced — light enough for a full day's shoot, yet substantial enough to inspire confidence. Buttons fall naturally under your fingers, the electronic viewfinder is crisp and immersive, and the tilting LCD screen invites you to experiment with angles. This is a camera designed not just to capture what's in front of you, but to make the process enjoyable.

With your battery charged, card inserted, and strap secured, you're ready to step into the world of image-making with one of Canon's most capable tools. In the next chapter, we'll get familiar with every button, dial, and menu so that your hands instinctively know what to do when the moment arrives.

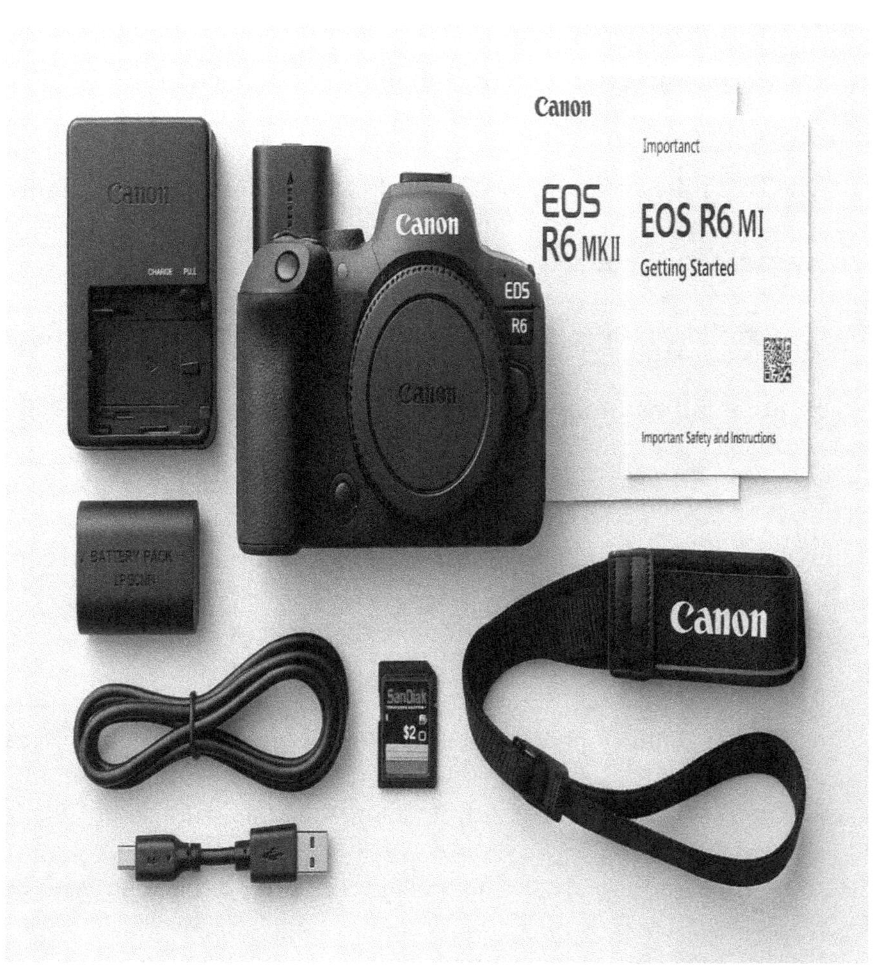

Canon
CHARGE PULL
BATTERY PACK
LP-E6NH
Canon
EOS
R6
SanDisk
32 G
Canon
Important
EOS
R6 MK II
Importanct
EOS R6 M I
Getting Started
Important Safety and Instructions

Chapter 2

Camera Layout & Controls Made Simple

When you first pick up the Canon EOS R6 Mark II, it can feel like there's a button or dial for everything — and in a way, there is. That's part of its charm and capability. The key is learning what each control does so you can stop fumbling and start shooting instinctively. Once you know where everything lives and how it works, the camera will feel like an extension of your hand, not a puzzle to solve.

Top View: Buttons, Dials, and Their Purposes

When you look down at the top of your R6 Mark II, you'll notice the layout is designed for both quick adjustments and comfortable handling.

- **Mode Dial** – This is your command center for changing shooting modes. From fully automatic settings for quick snapshots to manual control for artistic freedom, this dial is where you decide how much control you want over exposure. You'll find options like Auto, Program (P), Aperture Priority (Av), Shutter Priority (Tv), Manual (M), and customizable modes (C1, C2, C3) for your personal settings.

- **Main Control Dial (near the shutter button)** – This wheel lets you adjust shutter speed in manual or semi-automatic modes, or cycle through options depending on your shooting mode.

- **Shutter Button** – Positioned comfortably for your index finger, this is your photo trigger. Press halfway to lock focus and exposure; press fully to take the shot.

- **Movie Record Button** – A small, distinct button near the mode dial starts and stops video recording instantly, no matter what mode you're in.

- **Multi-Function (M-Fn) Button** – Right next to the shutter button, this lets you cycle quickly through assigned settings like ISO, white balance, or drive mode without diving into menus.

- **On/Off Switch** – Simple but essential — it powers the camera and is positioned for quick access with your thumb.

- **Top LCD Panel (if equipped)** – Displays quick status info such as shooting mode, shutter speed, aperture, ISO, and battery life at a glance.

Rear View: LCD, Buttons, and Quick Control Dial

Flip the camera around and you'll see the heart of your interaction with it — the screen and control buttons.

- **Electronic Viewfinder (EVF)** – Offers a real-time digital preview of your shot, including exposure, white balance, and focus indicators. Great for bright light shooting.

- **Vari-Angle LCD Screen** – Fully articulating, allowing you to shoot from high angles, low angles, or even face the screen forward for selfies or vlogging.

- **Quick Control Dial (rear wheel)** – Located just behind the thumb rest, this dial changes aperture in manual modes, navigates menus, or cycles through images in playback.

- **Multi-Controller Joystick** – Lets you move focus points or navigate menus quickly.

- **AF-On Button** – Used for back-button focusing — a favorite among experienced photographers who want to separate focusing from the shutter button.

- **Menu and Info Buttons** – Access the full menu system or toggle the amount of information shown on the screen.

- **Playback and Delete Buttons** – For reviewing and managing your images on the spot.

Side Panels: Ports and Connections

On either side of the camera body, you'll find ports hidden behind rubberized flaps to keep dust and moisture out.

- **Left Side** (most common port location):

  - **Microphone Input** – For plugging in external mics to improve audio quality.

  - **Headphone Jack** – Lets you monitor audio while recording video.

  - **USB-C Port** – For data transfer, charging (if supported), or tethered shooting.

  - **HDMI Micro Out** – Connects to external monitors or recorders for a bigger viewing experience.

  - **Remote Control Terminal** – For attaching a wired remote shutter release.

- **Right Side**:

- o **Dual SD Card Slots** – Allow you to either back up photos instantly or separate stills and video files for better organization.

Touchscreen Navigation Tips for Beginners and Seniors

Canon has designed the R6 Mark II's touchscreen to be intuitive, especially if you're familiar with smartphones or tablets.

- **Touch-to-Focus** – Tap anywhere on the screen to set your focus point instantly. This is faster than using the joystick for many situations.

- **Menu Scrolling** – Swipe up or down with your finger to move through settings. The touch response is fluid and responsive, so you won't feel stuck in the buttons-only era.

- **Quick Settings Screen (Q Button)** – Tapping the Q button (on-screen or physical) opens a simplified menu for the most frequently used settings, like ISO, drive mode, and white balance.

- **Pinch-to-Zoom in Playback** – Review your shots by pinching to zoom in and check details, just like you would on a smartphone.

- **Large Font Display Option** – For seniors or anyone who prefers easier readability, you can enlarge the on-screen text from the display settings.

Learning the camera layout is like learning the controls of a new car — the first few drives require you to look down, but soon you'll adjust settings without breaking eye contact with your subject. The Canon EOS R6 Mark II rewards this familiarity with speed, precision, and confidence in every shot.

TOP VIEW: BUTTONS, DIALS, AND THEIR PURPOSES

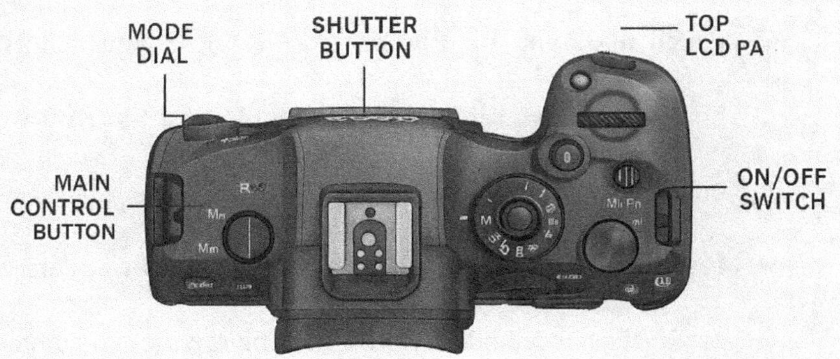

REAR VIEW: LCD, BUTTONS, AND QUICK CONTROL DIAL

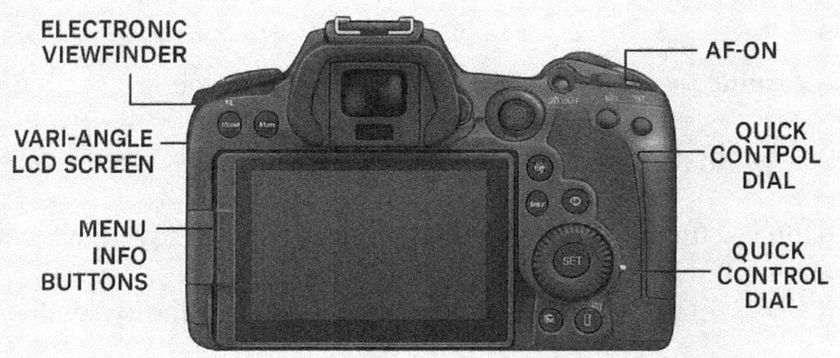

SIDE PANELS: PORTS AND CONNECTIONS

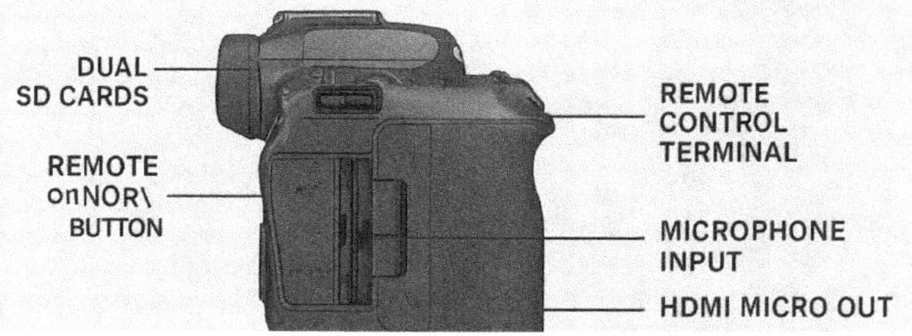

Chapter 3

Essential Camera Setup for Beginners & Seniors

A new camera feels most intimidating when the menus and settings are unfamiliar. The good news is, you don't have to learn everything at once. By setting up a few key functions right from the start, your Canon EOS R6 Mark II will feel more personal, easier to navigate, and far quicker to respond when you're trying to capture that perfect shot. This chapter is about turning the camera from "new and complex" into "comfortable and intuitive."

Setting Date, Time, Language, and Display Options

When you first turn on the R6 Mark II, it will prompt you to set the basics. These may seem minor, but they make your shooting smoother later — especially if you're organizing images or sharing them online.

1. **Date and Time –**

    Use the touchscreen or control dials to set your current date and time. This metadata is stored with every image and becomes invaluable when sorting or finding photos later. For travelers, enable Auto Time Update (if available) so the camera syncs with GPS or your phone when connected.

2. **Language –**

    Choose your preferred menu language. For seniors or those who feel more confident in their native language, this simple step makes exploring the camera much less intimidating.

3. **Display Brightness and Color Tone –**

    Adjust LCD brightness so it's comfortable for your eyes. If you shoot outdoors often, increase brightness; for low-light shooting, reduce it to avoid eye strain. You can also choose a warmer or cooler color tone for the display if you prefer a softer look.

4. **Viewfinder Display Preferences** –

Decide whether you want the electronic viewfinder to display a clean, minimal image or detailed information like exposure settings, histograms, and focus points. Many beginners prefer a simpler view until they get comfortable with manual adjustments.

Turning On Focus Peaking and Grid Lines

Two visual aids can dramatically improve your shooting confidence — especially if you're new to manual focusing or composition.

- **Focus Peaking** –

  This feature outlines the edges of your in-focus subject with a colored highlight (commonly red, yellow, or blue). It's incredibly useful for manual focus, macro shots, or filming video where autofocus might hunt.

  How to turn it on: Navigate to the AF menu, find "Focus

Peaking," enable it, and choose a highlight color that's easy for your eyes to see.

- **Grid Lines –**

  Grid lines help you compose shots with better balance. They're especially helpful for aligning horizons, keeping verticals straight in architecture, or following the rule of thirds.

  How to turn it on: In the display settings, choose "Grid Display" and select your preferred grid style. A simple rule-of-thirds grid works well for most situations.

Simplifying Menus with the My Menu Function

Canon's menu system is logical, but it's deep — too deep when you only use a few settings regularly. The My Menu function lets you create a shortcut menu with only the options you personally use.

1. Go to the green "My Menu" tab in the main menu.

2. Select "Add My Menu Tab" and choose "Register Settings."

3. Add frequently used options such as ISO range, white balance, image quality, or format card.

4. Once set up, you can jump directly to this personalized menu anytime, avoiding the need to dig through multiple layers of settings.

For seniors or anyone who wants minimal fuss, this feature keeps the camera feeling friendly and uncluttered.

Customizing Buttons for Faster Shooting

One of the most powerful ways to make the R6 Mark II feel like your camera is to assign functions to buttons that fit your shooting style. This customization means you can change key settings without removing your eye from the viewfinder.

- **Back-Button Focus (AF-ON)** – Many photographers prefer assigning autofocus to the AF-ON button instead of the shutter. This allows you to focus once and recompose without the camera trying to refocus when you press the shutter.

- **ISO Control** – Assign ISO adjustment to a dial or button for instant exposure changes in varying light.

- **Switching Between Eye/Face Detection and Manual Point Selection** – A great option if you alternate between portrait shooting and more controlled compositions.

- **Movie Record Button in Still Mode** – If you shoot video unexpectedly, you can assign the movie record button to trigger another function when not in video mode.

To customize buttons, head into the Setup Menu, look for Customize Buttons, and assign your preferred functions. Start small — two or three custom buttons are enough at first. As you grow more comfortable, you can fine-tune further.

Setting up your Canon EOS R6 Mark II this way is like arranging your workspace — once everything is in the right place, you can focus on creating rather than searching for the right tool. These changes might seem simple, but they'll save you time, reduce

frustration, and help you feel in control from the moment you switch

the camera on.

Part II: Mastering Photography

Chapter 4

Understanding Exposure on the R6 Mark II

Light is the raw material of every photograph. The Canon EOS R6 Mark II gives you powerful tools to control how light is captured, but to use them well, you need to understand exposure — the balance between light entering the camera and how the sensor records it.

In this chapter, we'll break down the exposure triangle — aperture, shutter speed, and ISO — and show how your R6 Mark II makes mastering this balance easier through exposure simulation in the viewfinder and quick adjustments like exposure compensation.

The Exposure Triangle: Aperture, Shutter

Speed, ISO

Think of exposure as a three-legged stool. If one leg changes, you must adjust the other two to keep the stool level. Each "leg" of the exposure triangle affects both how bright your image appears and how it looks creatively.

1. Aperture – The Lens Opening

Aperture controls the size of the opening in your lens through which light passes. On your R6 Mark II, it's measured in f-stops (e.g., f/1.8, f/4, f/11).

- **Wide Aperture (low f-number)** – e.g., f/2.8 lets in more light, ideal for low-light situations and creating a soft, blurred background (shallow depth of field).

- **Narrow Aperture (high f-number)** – e.g., f/11 lets in less light, ideal for landscapes where you want everything from front to back in sharp focus.

On the R6 Mark II: In Aperture Priority (Av) mode, you set the aperture and the camera selects the shutter speed. Turn the rear control dial to adjust it quickly.

2. Shutter Speed – The Time Light Hits the Sensor

Shutter speed determines how long the camera's shutter stays open.

- **Fast Shutter Speeds** (e.g., 1/1000 sec) freeze action, perfect for sports or wildlife.
- **Slow Shutter Speeds** (e.g., 1/4 sec) create motion blur, great for silky waterfalls or light trails.

On the R6 Mark II: In Shutter Priority (Tv) mode, turn the main control dial near the shutter button to change shutter speed. The camera automatically adjusts aperture.

3. ISO – Sensor Sensitivity

ISO adjusts the sensor's sensitivity to light.

- **Low ISO (100–400)** produces the cleanest images with minimal noise, best for bright conditions.

- **High ISO (3200 and above)** allows you to shoot in darker conditions but introduces more digital grain.

On the R6 Mark II: You can change ISO quickly by pressing the ISO button or assigning it to a control dial for instant access.

The Balancing Act: If you open the aperture to let in more light, you may need a faster shutter speed or lower ISO to avoid overexposure. If you raise ISO, you can use a faster shutter speed in low light, but you'll trade off image cleanliness.

Exposure Simulation in the Viewfinder

One of the greatest advantages of the EOS R6 Mark II's electronic viewfinder (EVF) is exposure simulation — the ability to preview exactly how your settings will affect the final image before you press the shutter.

When exposure simulation is turned on:

- As you adjust aperture, shutter speed, or ISO, the viewfinder brightens or darkens to reflect the resulting exposure.

- You'll see live depth-of-field effects when adjusting aperture.

- In low-light situations, the EVF can amplify the scene so you can still compose easily, even when it's darker than the final image will appear.

Tip: If you're shooting in very low light with exposure simulation on, you might notice the display becomes bright even though your settings will produce a dark photo. In these cases, check your histogram or meter reading to confirm exposure accuracy.

How to Use Exposure Compensation

Even in automatic or semi-automatic modes, the camera's built-in metering might not always produce the brightness you want. That's where exposure compensation comes in — a quick way to make your image lighter or darker without fully switching to manual mode.

- **Positive Exposure Compensation (+)** – Brightens the image. Useful when your subject is against a bright background, like a person in front of snow or a white wall, where the camera might underexpose.

- **Negative Exposure Compensation (–)** – Darkens the image. Handy when photographing bright scenes with lots of light areas, such as sunlit beaches or white clothing, where highlights risk blowing out.

On the R6 Mark II:

- In Av or Tv mode, simply turn the quick control dial while pressing the exposure compensation button (or just turn it if exposure comp is assigned to a dial).

- Watch the EVF or LCD preview update in real time so you can dial in just the right brightness.

Practical Example

Imagine you're photographing your child running across a sunlit park:

1. You want to freeze the action → choose Shutter Priority (Tv) and set 1/1000 sec.

2. The camera selects the aperture automatically, but the image looks a bit dark.

3. You dial in +0.7 exposure compensation and watch the preview brighten.

4. You take the shot, confident that both the motion is frozen and the exposure looks perfect.

Mastering the exposure triangle is less about memorizing numbers and more about recognizing how changes affect your image's look and feel. With the R6 Mark II's exposure simulation, you can see those changes live, which makes learning faster and shooting more intuitive.

Understanding Exposure on the R6 Mark II

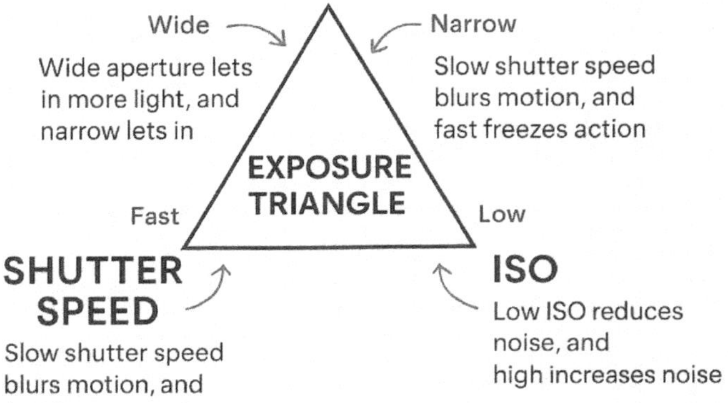

Exposure Simulation in the Viewfinder

The viewfinder preview exposure exposure as you adjust settings

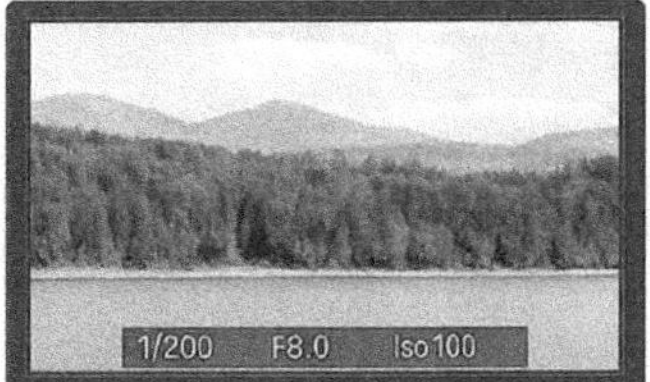

How to Use Exposure Compensation

Adjust exposure to brighten or darken your images

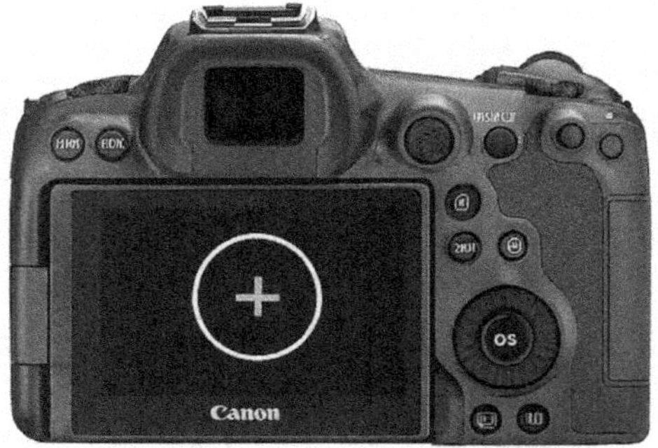

Chapter 5

Autofocus Like a Pro

One of the reasons photographers fall in love with the Canon EOS R6 Mark II is its autofocus system. It's not just fast — it's smart. It can track a bird in flight, follow a bride walking down the aisle, or lock onto an actor's eye in a dimly lit scene. But to get that performance every time, you need to understand how the autofocus modes work and how to use them in real-world situations.

This chapter takes you deep into the R6 Mark II's AF capabilities so you can go beyond "let the camera figure it out" and start taking control.

AF Area Modes Explained

The R6 Mark II offers different autofocus area modes — each suited for specific subjects and shooting conditions. Knowing when to use each is the difference between nailing the shot and missing it.

Spot AF

- Uses a very small focus area, perfect for precise work like macro photography or focusing through busy foregrounds.

- Best used when you have time to compose and your subject is still.

- Example: Focusing on a single flower petal or a subject's eye when shooting close-up portraits.

1-Point AF (Single)

- Focuses using a single point you can position anywhere in the frame.

- Great for portraits, landscapes, or product shots where you
  want exact control over the focal plane.

- Example: Placing the AF point on a person's nearest eye in
  a controlled environment.

Zone AF

- Divides the frame into a selectable "zone" where the camera
  looks for focus.

- Good for moving subjects that you can keep within a certain
  area of the frame.

- Example: Photographing a child running across a yard —
  you don't need pinpoint precision, just focus within the
  action zone.

Tracking AF (Whole Area with Subject Tracking)

- The camera automatically detects and tracks a subject across
  the frame, even if it moves unpredictably.

- Works exceptionally well with the R6 Mark II's subject detection modes (face, eye, and animal).

- Example: A soccer player weaving through opponents or a bird changing direction mid-flight.

Tip: In fast-paced shooting, start with Tracking AF and let the camera's intelligent system follow your subject. In controlled conditions, switch to 1-Point AF or Spot AF for maximum precision.

Eye, Face, and Animal Detection AF

Canon's deep learning technology gives the R6 Mark II uncanny subject recognition abilities.

Eye Detection AF

- Locks onto a subject's eye and keeps it in sharp focus, even if they move slightly.

- Essential for portrait, wedding, and street photographers who want the sharpest possible eye detail.

- Works in both stills and video.

Face Detection AF

- Expands detection to an entire face, useful when the subject is further away or wearing glasses, hats, or masks that partially obscure the eyes.

- Automatically switches to Eye Detection when close enough.

Animal Detection AF

- Designed for wildlife and pet photography.

- Recognizes dogs, cats, and birds, locking onto eyes or heads even when they move unpredictably.

- Works well for tracking birds in flight — a major advantage for nature photographers.

Pro Insight: When photographing animals or active children, use Animal Detection or Face/Eye Detection in combination with Tracking AF. This way, if your subject turns away or moves erratically, the camera continues to follow them without losing focus.

Using Back-Button Focus for Consistency

One of the most effective ways to improve your focusing workflow is to separate the act of focusing from the act of taking the photo — known as back-button focus.

How It Works

- Normally, pressing the shutter button halfway both focuses and meters the scene.

- With back-button focus, you reassign autofocus to the AF-ON button on the back of the camera.

- This means pressing the shutter only takes the picture — focus is controlled independently.

Why It's Better

- Prevents the camera from refocusing every time you press the shutter, which is useful when recomposing.

- Gives you faster reactions in sports or wildlife photography — you can focus once and keep shooting without the camera hunting.

- Reduces missed moments when the subject is moving erratically but remains in the same focal plane.

Setting It Up on the R6 Mark II

1. Go to the Custom Functions menu.

2. Select "Customize Buttons."

3. Set the AF-ON button to start autofocus.

4. Disable autofocus from the shutter button.

5. Practice: Hold the AF-ON button with your thumb to focus, then release and shoot at will.

Once you get used to back-button focusing, it feels natural — and you'll wonder how you ever worked without it.

Practical Shooting Scenario

You're photographing your dog running across a field:

1. Set AF Area to Tracking AF.

2. Enable Animal Detection.

3. Use back-button focus to start tracking before the dog even reaches you.

4. As the dog runs, the camera keeps the eyes sharp while you focus solely on timing your shots.

The result? Crisp, sharp eyes in every frame, even at 12 frames per second.

The Canon EOS R6 Mark II's autofocus system isn't just a tool — it's an ally. By understanding AF area modes, enabling smart detection, and adopting back-button focus, you can shoot with speed, precision, and confidence in almost any situation.

AF AREA MODES EXPLAINED

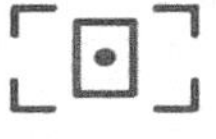

Spot AF

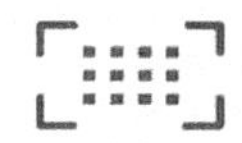

Single AF

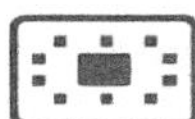

Tracking AF

Tracking AF

EYE/FACE/ANIMAL DETECTION AF

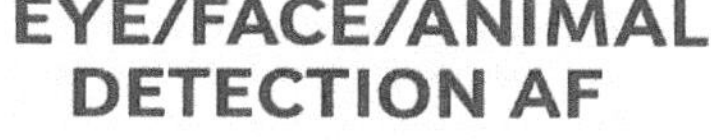

BACK-BUTTON FOCUS

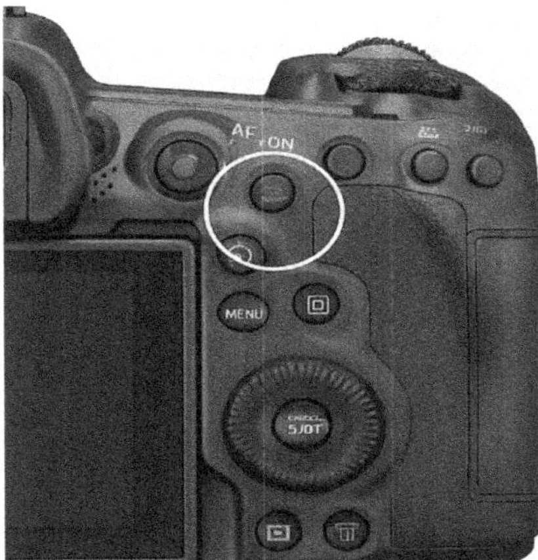

USING BACK-BUTTON FOCUS

Using back-button focus for consistency

AF area modes explanation

Eye detection AF

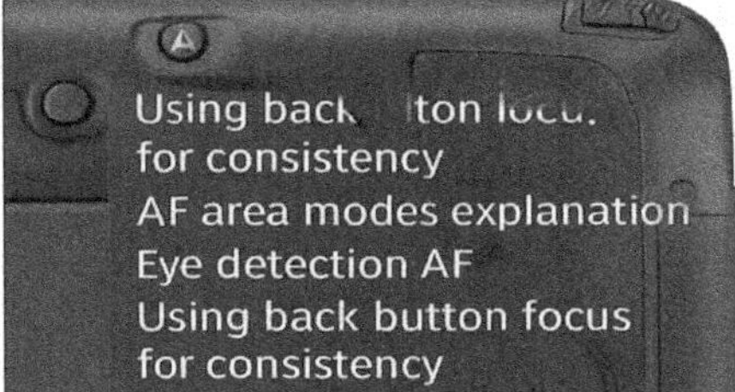

Chapter 6

Perfecting Image Quality

Great photography isn't only about sharp focus or balanced exposure — it's also about delivering images that look rich, accurate, and true to your creative vision. On the Canon EOS R6 Mark II, image quality is shaped by three core choices: file format (RAW vs. JPEG), Picture Styles, and white balance. Understanding and mastering these settings ensures that the photographs you take are exactly how you imagined them — whether straight out of the camera or after editing.

RAW vs. JPEG Shooting

When you press the shutter, your R6 Mark II captures far more data than you might realize. The choice between RAW and JPEG determines how much of that data is saved — and how much flexibility you have later.

RAW

- A RAW file is like a digital film negative. It contains all the data your sensor captured, without compression or heavy in-camera processing.

- **Advantages:**

  - Maximum detail and dynamic range.

  - Greater control in post-processing for exposure, white balance, and color correction.

  - Better recovery of shadows and highlights in editing software.

- **Considerations:**

  - Larger file sizes (can be 3–5× bigger than JPEGs).

  - Requires processing in software like Adobe Lightroom, Capture One, or Canon's Digital Photo Professional before sharing or printing.

JPEG

- JPEGs are processed and compressed in-camera, ready to use straight away.

- **Advantages:**

  o Smaller file sizes — easier for storage and faster for sharing.

  o Immediate usability without editing.

  o Good for casual shooting or events where quick turnaround is important.

- **Considerations:**

  o Less editing flexibility.

  o Compression can cause loss of detail and color information.

Pro Tip: If you want the best of both worlds, set your R6 Mark II to RAW + JPEG. This way, you have a ready-to-use JPEG and a RAW file for critical edits.

Picture Styles: Standard, Neutral, and Fine Detail

Picture Styles control how the camera processes colors, contrast, and sharpness before saving the image (especially for JPEGs and video). Even though RAW files can override most of these settings during editing, Picture Styles still affect your in-camera preview and video output.

Standard

- Balanced for everyday shooting.

- Produces vivid colors, moderate contrast, and pleasing sharpness.

- Ideal for portraits, landscapes, and general photography where you want lively, ready-to-use images.

Neutral

- Flatter tones, lower contrast, and less saturation.

- Keeps details in highlights and shadows, making it ideal for post-processing work where you want maximum flexibility.

- Excellent for professional workflows where you'll color grade images later.

Fine Detail

- Prioritizes maximum sharpness and clarity, bringing out textures.

- Great for macro photography, product shots, architecture, and landscapes where surface detail matters.

- Can make portraits look overly sharp, so use with care when photographing skin.

Pro Insight: Even if you shoot RAW, using an appropriate Picture Style can help you visualize your final image more accurately in the viewfinder.

White Balance for Accurate Colors

White balance (WB) ensures the colors in your photo look natural by compensating for the color temperature of the light source.

Auto White Balance (AWB)

- The camera automatically detects the lighting and corrects colors.

- Works well in most conditions, especially in mixed lighting environments.

- Modern AWB in the R6 Mark II is excellent at preserving natural skin tones.

Preset White Balance Options

- **Daylight** – Slightly warm, perfect for sunny outdoor shooting.

- **Cloudy** – Warms up the image to counteract cool overcast light.

- **Tungsten** – Corrects strong orange indoor lighting.

- **Fluorescent** – Reduces greenish tints under certain artificial lights.

Custom White Balance

- Use a white or gray card under your shooting light to set the most accurate color balance possible.

- Essential for product photography, fashion shoots, or any scenario where exact color accuracy matters.

Pro Tip: For consistent results, especially in controlled environments like studios, set a custom white balance instead of relying on AWB.

Practical Workflow for Maximum Quality

Imagine you're photographing a high-end watch for a magazine feature:

1. Set file format to RAW for maximum editing flexibility.

2. Choose Fine Detail Picture Style to capture the texture of the watch face and band.

3. Set a custom white balance using a gray card under your lighting setup.

4. Capture the shots knowing that every detail, tone, and color is accurate and ready for professional post-production.

Perfecting image quality on the Canon EOS R6 Mark II is about making informed choices before you press the shutter. By understanding your file format, selecting the right Picture Style, and dialing in accurate white balance, you're not just taking pictures — you're creating images with lasting impact.

RAW VS. JPEG SHOOTING

- Highest quality
- More editing flexibility
- Larger file size

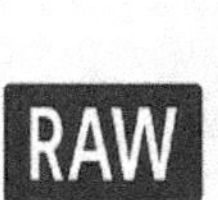

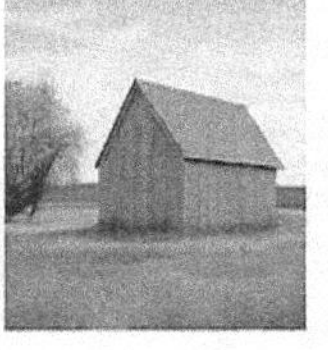

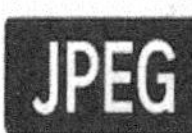

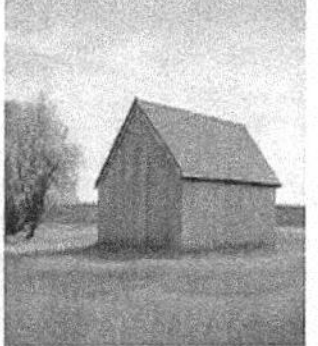

PICTURE STYLES WHEN TO USE

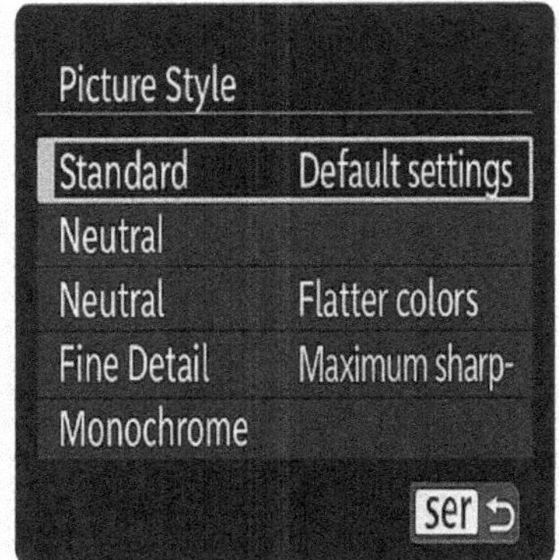

WHITE BALANCE FOR ACCURATE COLORS

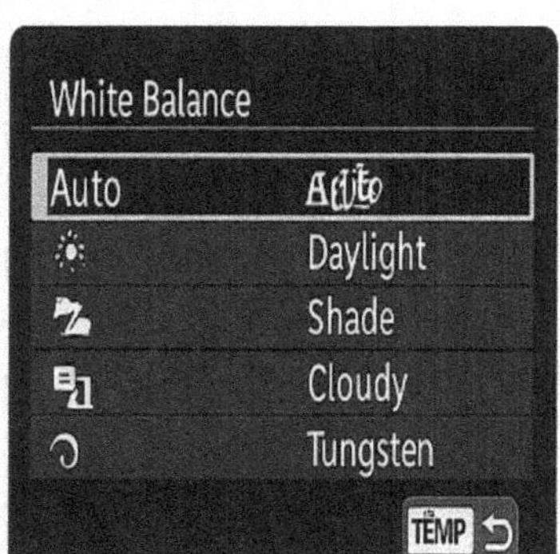

AWB = ☀ Daylight

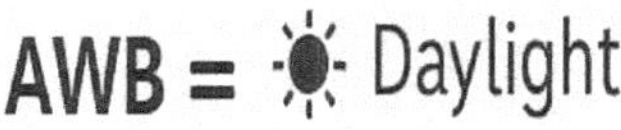

   🔦 Shade

   ☁ Cloudy

   💡 Tungsten

   ≪ White

A   K Custom

Chapter 7

Shooting Scenarios for Stunning Results

One of the most exciting things about the Canon EOS R6 Mark II is how adaptable it is. From fast-paced sports to quiet landscapes, it's capable of producing images that are not only technically excellent but also emotionally compelling.

The key is knowing how to tailor your settings, lens choice, and technique to the scene in front of you. In this chapter, we'll walk through four common but very different shooting scenarios — each with tips to help you make the most of your camera's strengths.

Portraits: Lighting and Lens Choices

Portraits are about more than just capturing someone's likeness — they're about revealing personality, mood, and connection. Your lens choice, lighting, and camera settings all play a part.

Lens Choices for Portraits

- 85mm or 50mm prime lenses are classics for portraits. They create flattering perspective and allow you to shoot with wide apertures for a beautifully blurred background.

- For environmental portraits where you want to include more of the surroundings, a 35mm lens works beautifully.

Lighting Considerations

- **Natural Light:** Soft, diffused light from a cloudy day or a shaded spot can be magical for skin tones.

- **Golden Hour:** The warm, low-angle light just after sunrise or before sunset adds dimension and atmosphere.

- **Artificial Light:** If indoors, use a softbox or bounced flash to avoid harsh shadows.

Camera Settings

- Aperture Priority (Av mode) with a wide aperture like f/2.8 or wider for subject isolation.
- Eye Detection AF enabled to keep eyes sharp, even if the subject moves slightly.
- ISO low (100–400) for the cleanest image quality.

Action & Sports: Freeze vs. Motion Blur

Capturing movement is a test of both timing and settings. The R6 Mark II's rapid burst speed and advanced autofocus tracking give you a big advantage.

Freezing Action

- Use Shutter Priority (Tv) mode.

- Start at 1/1000 sec or faster for fast-moving subjects like sports players or wildlife.

- Tracking AF with subject detection will keep focus locked on moving subjects.

Motion Blur for Energy

- Slower shutter speeds (1/60 sec or even slower) can intentionally blur parts of the scene, creating a sense of movement.

- Pan with your subject while keeping them sharp against a blurred background — a great technique for motorsports or running events.

Other Tips

- Use continuous shooting mode to capture multiple frames in quick succession.

- Keep both eyes open when tracking unpredictable action — it helps with anticipation.

Landscapes: Using Depth-of-Field Creatively

Landscapes invite you to slow down and be deliberate, and the R6 Mark II rewards careful composition.

Depth-of-Field Choices

- For expansive scenes, use a narrow aperture (f/8–f/16) to keep both foreground and background sharp.
- For more artistic landscapes, open the aperture (f/4 or wider) to blur backgrounds and draw attention to specific elements, like a single flower in a meadow.

Composition Tips

- Use grid lines in your viewfinder to apply the rule of thirds.
- Include foreground interest for depth — rocks, plants, or leading lines that draw the eye into the frame.

Other Considerations

- Shoot during the golden hour for softer light and richer colors.

- Use a tripod for stability, especially if you're using slower shutter speeds for maximum depth-of-field.

Low-Light Shooting Without Excessive Noise

Low-light photography can be magical — city streets at night, candlelit dinners, or starry skies. But it's also where image noise can creep in.

Maximizing Light Without Raising ISO Too Much

- Use the widest aperture your lens allows (e.g., f/1.8 or f/2.8).

- Slow your shutter speed, but keep it fast enough to avoid camera shake — or use a tripod if the subject is stationary.

Leaning on R6 Mark II Features

- Enable In-Body Image Stabilization (IBIS) to handhold shots at slower shutter speeds.

- Use Animal or Eye Detection AF in dim environments to help the camera lock onto your subject quickly.

Post-Processing Note

- Shooting RAW allows you to apply noise reduction in editing software while preserving more detail.

A Final Note on Adapting

These scenarios are starting points. As you gain experience, you'll find yourself blending techniques — a portrait in low light, a landscape with a moving element, or an action shot with intentional blur. The beauty of the R6 Mark II is that it can handle all of them, as long as you give it the right instructions.

PORTRAITS
Lighting and Lens Choices

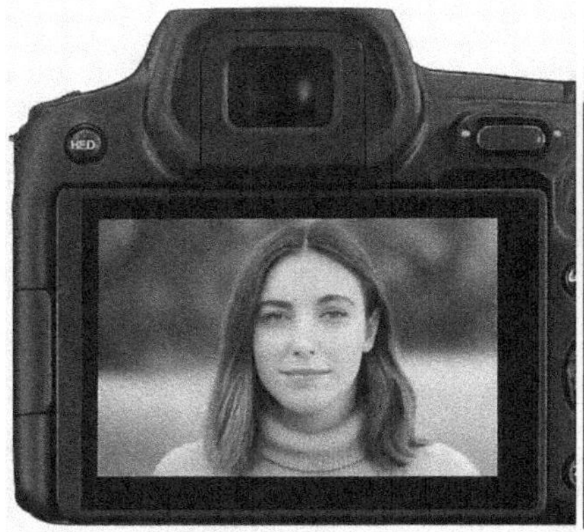

ACTION & SPORTS
Freeze vs. Motion Blur

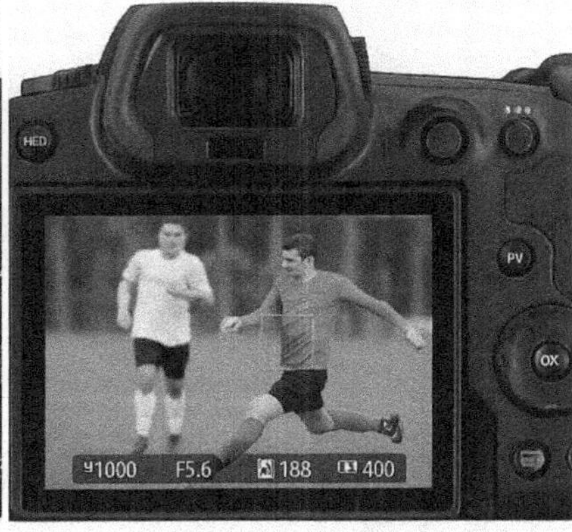

LANDSCAPES
Using Depth-of-Field Creatively

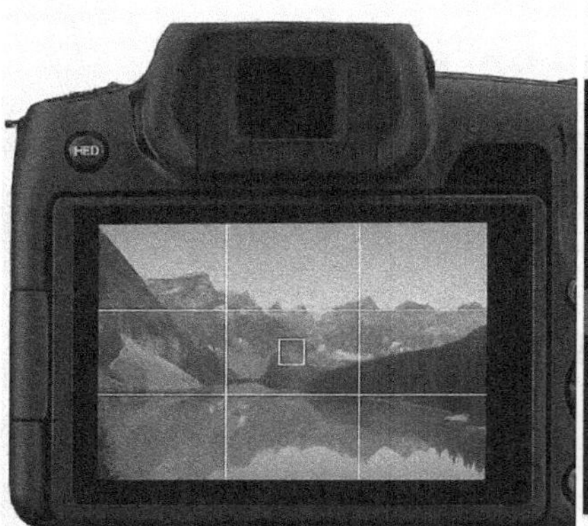

LOW LIGHT SHOOTING
Without Excessive Noise

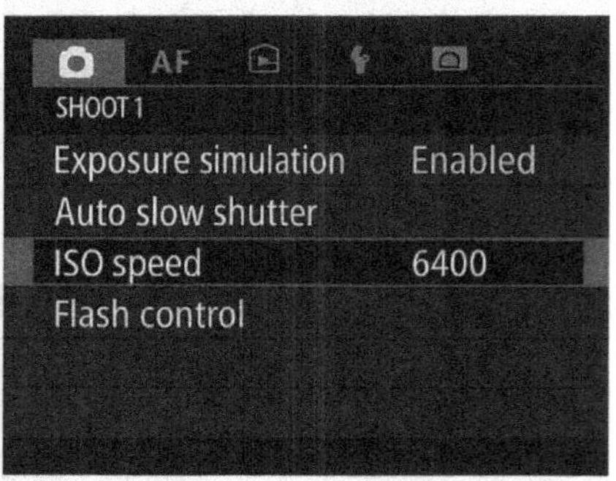

Part III: Cinematography & Video Mastery (Dedicated Section for Cinematography Category)

Chapter 8

Introduction to Video with the R6 Mark II

For filmmakers and content creators, the Canon EOS R6 Mark II is more than a stills camera that happens to shoot video — it's a hybrid powerhouse. It blends professional-level image quality with intuitive handling, making it equally comfortable on a wedding shoot, a YouTube set, or in the middle of a fast-paced documentary. Whether you're a seasoned videographer or just starting to explore motion, this chapter will help you understand why the R6 Mark II has earned such a loyal following in the filmmaking world, and how to set it up for success.

Why This Camera Is a Favorite for

Filmmakers

The R6 Mark II packs in features that rival much more expensive cinema cameras, while remaining compact and versatile.

- **6K Oversampled 4K Recording** – The camera uses its entire sensor to capture more detail than standard 4K, then downsamples for a sharper, cleaner final image.

- **High Frame Rates** – Record 4K at up to 60fps for smooth motion or slow it down in post-production, and Full HD at up to 180fps for ultra-slow motion shots.

- **Dual Pixel CMOS AF II** – Canon's autofocus system is trusted for its accuracy and subject tracking, crucial for video work where missed focus can ruin a take.

- **C-Log 3 Profile** – Gives you up to 12 stops of dynamic range, ideal for color grading and matching footage from cinema cameras.

- **Compact & Lightweight Body** – Easier to rig for gimbals, handheld work, or travel shoots compared to bulkier cinema setups.

- **Excellent Low-Light Performance** – Large sensor and strong ISO performance allow filming in dim environments with less noise.

For many filmmakers, this camera offers the perfect balance: cinema-quality footage without sacrificing portability or workflow speed.

Setting Up Movie Mode Correctly

Switching from stills to video on the R6 Mark II involves more than just flipping the mode dial — thoughtful setup ensures you get the best possible footage.

1. **Switch to Movie Mode**

o   Rotate the mode dial to the movie camera icon. This activates dedicated video menus and disables stills-only settings.

2. **Select Your Resolution and Frame Rate**

    o   For most work, 4K 24fps or 25fps delivers a cinematic look.

    o   For smoother motion or sports coverage, choose 4K 50/60fps.

    o   For slow motion, go with Full HD 120fps or 180fps.

3. **Choose a Picture Profile**

    o   C-Log 3 if you plan to color grade your footage for maximum dynamic range.

    o   Neutral or Standard for minimal post-processing.

4. **Set Shutter Speed for Video**

    o   Follow the 180-degree shutter rule: shutter speed should be roughly double your frame rate (e.g., 1/50 sec for 25fps, 1/120 sec for 60fps) for natural motion blur.

5. **Adjust ISO and Aperture**

   o   Keep ISO as low as possible for cleaner footage.

   o   Aperture choice depends on your depth-of-field needs — wide apertures for shallow depth, narrower for more of the scene in focus.

6. **Enable Subject Tracking AF**

   o   Eye, face, and animal detection work seamlessly in video, helping maintain sharp focus even during movement.

7. **Check Your Audio Levels**

   o   Use the on-screen audio meters to avoid distortion — keep peaks in the green to low yellow range.

Essential Accessories for Video Shooting

While the R6 Mark II can shoot excellent video straight out of the box, the right accessories can elevate your work, improve handling, and enhance audio/visual quality.

External Microphone

- The built-in mic is fine for reference audio, but for clean, professional sound, use a shotgun mic (like the Rode VideoMic NTG) or a wireless lavalier system for interviews.

Tripod or Monopod

- For locked-off shots, a sturdy tripod is a must. For mobile shooting, a monopod or fluid video head tripod allows smooth pans and tilts.

Gimbal Stabilizer

- Ideal for dynamic moving shots, walking sequences, or following subjects — a gimbal smooths out handheld shake.

ND Filters

- Neutral Density filters allow you to keep your shutter speed at cinematic values even in bright daylight, preventing overexposure without needing to stop down your aperture.

External Monitor/Recorder

- A monitor like the Atomos Ninja V lets you see your framing more clearly, record in higher-quality ProRes, and monitor exposure with advanced tools like waveforms and false color.

Extra Batteries and Storage

- Video recording drains power faster than stills — pack multiple LP-E6NH batteries and high-speed UHS-II SD cards for uninterrupted shooting.

Practical Example

Imagine filming a street food documentary:

- You set the R6 Mark II to 4K 25fps with C-Log 3 for grading flexibility.

- A shotgun mic captures the sizzling and vendor chatter with clarity.

- A gimbal keeps your tracking shots smooth as you follow a chef preparing dishes.

- ND filters let you shoot at f/2.8 in midday sunlight without overexposing.

- Back at the studio, your footage is crisp, cinematic, and ready for color grading.

The Canon EOS R6 Mark II offers filmmakers the ability to capture cinematic-quality video without the bulk of a full cinema rig. By setting up Movie Mode properly and equipping yourself with the right accessories, you can produce professional results whether you're working solo or as part of a crew.

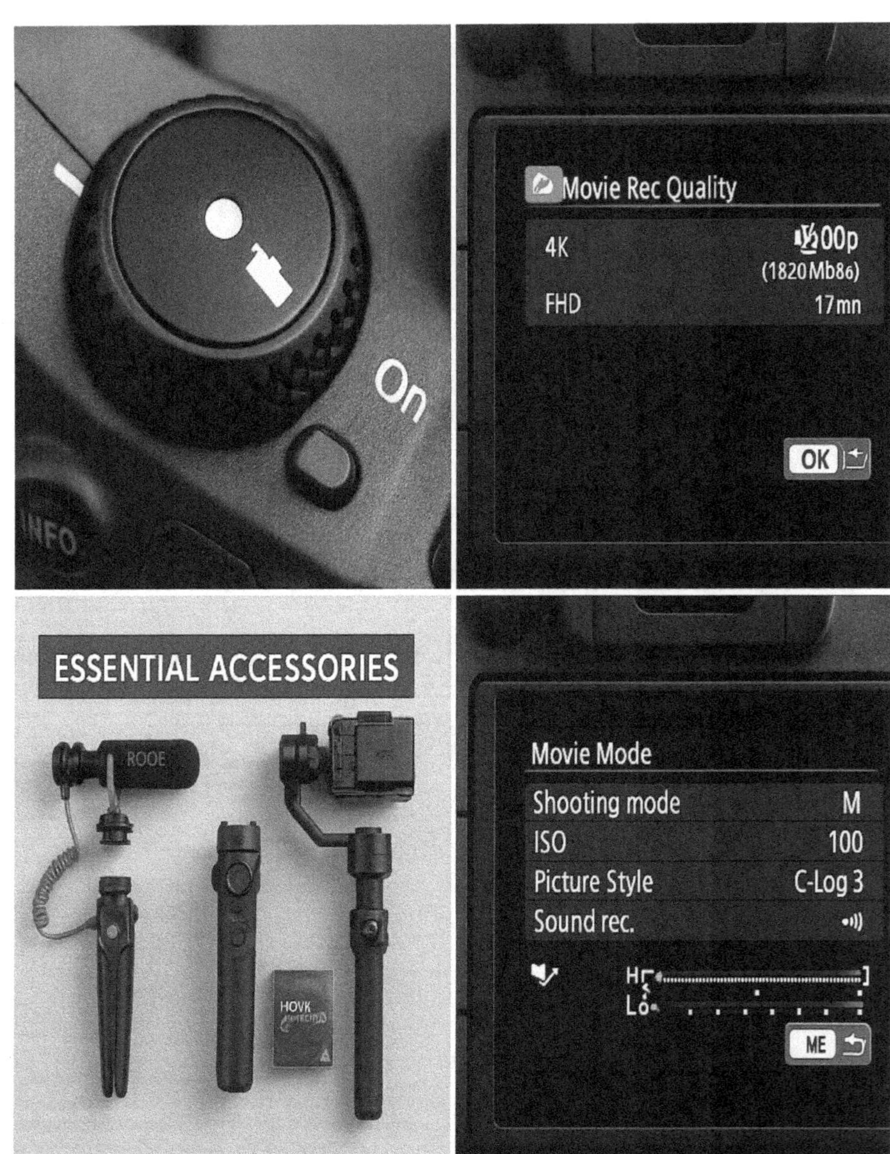
On
INFO
Movie Rec Quality
4K
(1820 Mb86)
FHD
17mn
OK
ESSENTIAL ACCESSORIES
ROOE
HOVK
Movie Mode
Shooting mode   M
ISO   100
Picture Style   C-Log 3
Sound rec.
Hi
Lo
ME

Chapter 9

4K & High-Resolution Recording Modes

The Canon EOS R6 Mark II isn't just a hybrid stills camera — it's a machine built for filmmakers who demand both flexibility and quality. One of its strongest selling points is its ability to record breathtaking 4K footage, not just at standard quality, but oversampled from its 6K sensor readout. Understanding these recording modes and compression options will give you the control to tailor your footage for any project, from fast-turnaround YouTube content to feature-length productions.

4K UHD and Oversampled 6K from the Sensor

The R6 Mark II offers two main approaches to 4K capture:

1. **Standard 4K UHD**

o   Captured directly at 3840 × 2160 pixels.

o   Faster processing, lower data rates, and ideal for projects that don't need extreme detail or for quick edits.

2. **Oversampled 4K from 6K**

o   The camera reads the full 6K width of the sensor, then downsamples the data to 4K resolution.

o   Produces sharper footage with more color information and reduced moiré.

o   This is the mode to use when maximum image quality is your priority, such as for cinematic work, commercials, or high-end client projects.

Oversampling is essentially like capturing with a super-high megapixel camera and then resizing the image down — it retains more detail and cleaner edges while minimizing aliasing.

Bitrates and Recording Formats Explained

When shooting video, bitrate determines how much data is recorded per second. Higher bitrates generally mean better quality but also larger file sizes.

- **Higher Bitrate (Up to 340 Mbps in 4K ALL-I)**

    o Preserves more detail in fast motion scenes.

    o Ideal for action, sports, and heavy grading in post.

- **Lower Bitrate (IPB 60–180 Mbps)**

    o Smaller file sizes, easier for storage and editing on slower computers.

    o Perfect for social media or quick client previews.

The R6 Mark II records in MP4 format with H.264 or H.265 codecs, giving you wide compatibility with editing programs.

Choosing Between IPB and ALL-I

Compression

The two main compression methods on the R6 Mark II offer different strengths:

- **IPB (Interframe)**
    - Compresses by storing only the changes between frames rather than each full frame.
    - Smaller file sizes, longer recording times.
    - Slightly more processor-heavy when editing.
    - Best for projects where you need to record for long periods or conserve storage.

- **ALL-I (Intra-frame)**
    - Records every single frame individually.
    - Larger file sizes, shorter recording times.
    - Easier to edit and more robust in post-production, especially for heavy color grading or VFX.
    - Best for professional projects and high-motion scenes.

Pro Tip:

If you're shooting a wedding ceremony or a long interview, IPB might be your go-to for storage efficiency. But if you're creating a music video with lots of fast cuts and effects, ALL-I will make post-production smoother.

Practical Workflow Example

Imagine you're shooting a short film:

- You choose oversampled 4K for maximum sharpness.

- You set the camera to ALL-I for easy frame-by-frame editing.

- You record at a high bitrate to preserve every shadow and highlight detail for grading.

- The footage comes out cinematic, clean, and ready to handle color adjustments without falling apart.

With its oversampled 6K-to-4K recording and versatile bitrate options, the Canon EOS R6 Mark II gives you the creative freedom to balance quality, storage, and editing performance. By understanding and selecting the right recording mode for each job, you'll be able to deliver footage that matches — and often exceeds — professional standards.

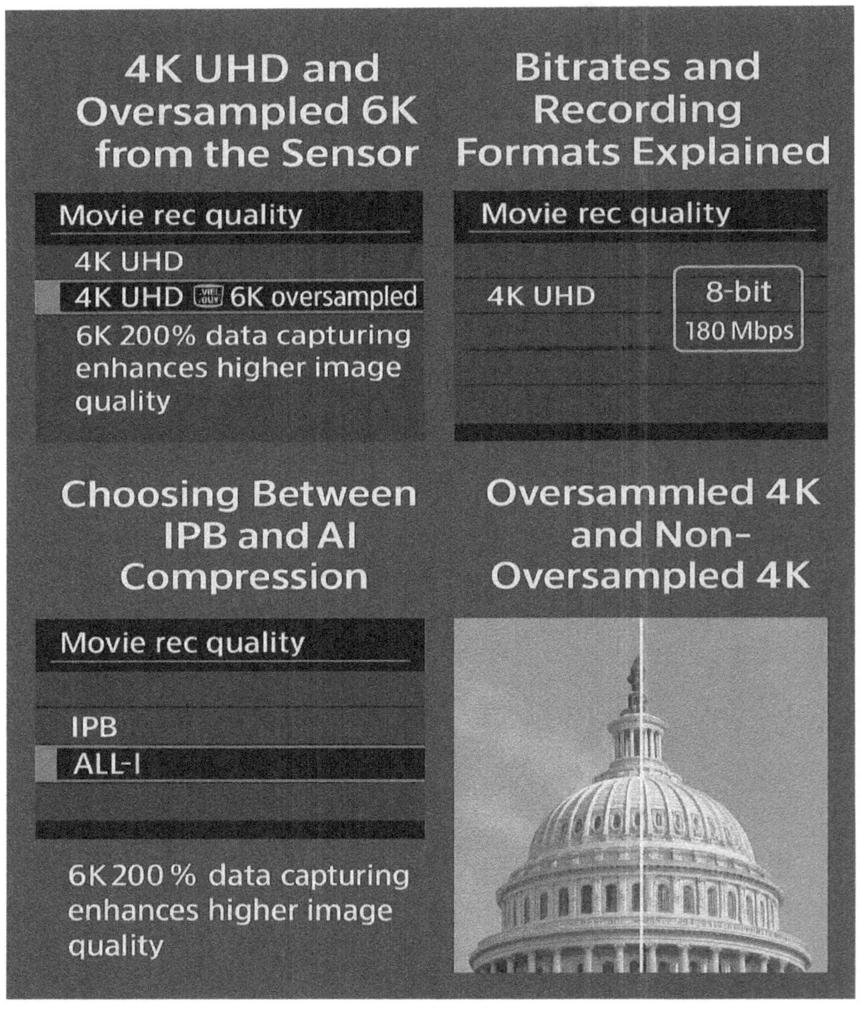

Chapter 10

Frame Rates for Cinematic Motion

One of the most overlooked yet powerful creative tools in filmmaking is your choice of frame rate. While resolution determines how sharp your video looks, frame rate defines *how* motion is portrayed. On the Canon EOS R6 Mark II, you have a range of frame rates at your disposal, each carrying its own emotional and technical qualities. Mastering this will let you create videos that not only look professional but also *feel* exactly how you want them to.

24p – For Film-Like Motion

24 frames per second is the gold standard for cinema. This is the frame rate most movies have been shot at for nearly a century, and it's what our brains associate with a "film look." The slightly lower

frame count produces a gentle motion blur, giving movement a smooth, organic quality that feels natural on the big screen.

On the R6 Mark II:

- Shooting in 24p is perfect for narrative work — short films, documentaries, or any project where you want that classic, immersive storytelling vibe.
- Pair 24p with a shutter speed of 1/48 or 1/**50** for the most cinematic motion blur.

Pro Tip: If you want your YouTube travel vlog to feel like a short film, switching to 24p will instantly give it that rich, cinematic mood.

30p – For Web and Broadcast Content

30 frames per second (technically 29.97p in NTSC regions) is a great all-rounder for online platforms. It offers a touch more clarity in motion than 24p while still looking natural to most viewers.

On the R6 Mark II:

- Ideal for talking-head videos, interviews, product reviews, and most content that will live primarily on the web.
- Works well for mixed projects where some footage might be broadcast on TV, which often prefers 30p in certain regions.

Pro Tip: If you're mixing slow-motion shots with regular footage, shooting in 30p can make speed ramping to 60p smoother and more consistent.

60p – For Smooth Motion and Action

60 frames per second offers ultra-smooth playback, perfect for sports, fast-moving events, or scenes where motion clarity is critical. The extra frames reduce motion blur, making it easier for the viewer to follow rapid movement.

On the R6 Mark II:

- Essential for capturing dance performances, wildlife in motion, or high-energy sports events.

- Gives a "live broadcast" feel — crisp, detailed, and fluid.

- Can be slowed down by 50% on a 30p timeline for subtle slow-motion effects.

Pro Tip: Avoid overusing 60p for cinematic work — the ultra-smooth look can sometimes feel too "real" and take away the magic of film-like storytelling.

120fps – For Slow-Motion Magic

The R6 Mark II can record 120 frames per second in Full HD, allowing you to slow footage down by a factor of five on a 24p timeline. This turns everyday moments into visually stunning sequences — water splashing, hair blowing in the wind, or the explosive movement of an athlete in mid-action.

On the R6 Mark II:

- Best used for creative inserts in action scenes, wedding highlights, or nature documentaries.

- Shooting at 120fps requires good lighting — higher frame rates demand faster shutter speeds, which means less light hitting the sensor.

Pro Tip: Use slow motion sparingly. When every shot is slowed down, the novelty wears off. Reserve it for moments you truly want the audience to savor.

Matching Frame Rate to Story

Think of frame rates as part of your storytelling toolkit:

- 24p = *Emotion and immersion*

- 30p = *Balance and clarity*

- 60p = *Energy and action*

- 120fps = *Drama and artistry*

By being intentional about frame rate, you can control not only how your footage looks but how it *feels* to the viewer.

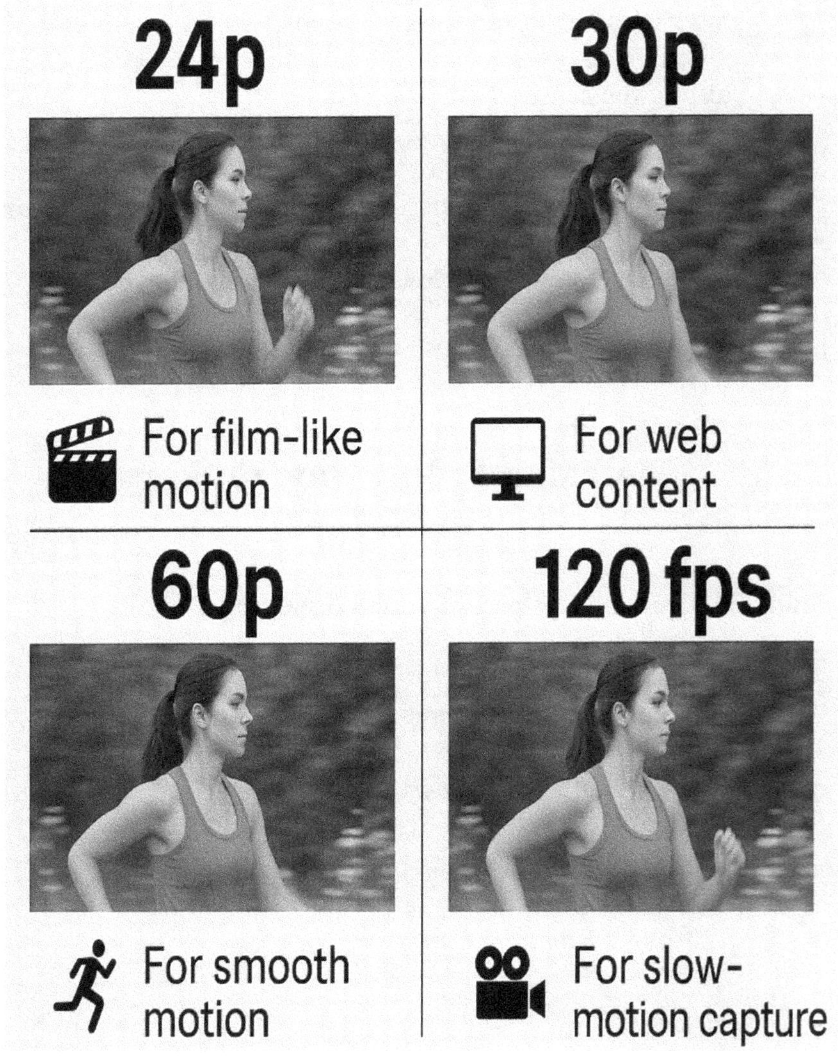

Chapter 11

Color Profiles & Grading Workflows

Color isn't just a technical setting—it's the emotional language of your video. The Canon EOS R6 Mark II gives you several ways to shape that language, from built-in picture styles to professional log profiles designed for advanced color grading. Understanding these options will help you control the look of your footage right from the moment you press record.

Standard, Neutral, and Canon Log 3 Explained

Standard

This is Canon's all-purpose color profile, tuned for pleasing skin tones, vibrant yet natural colors, and solid contrast straight out of the camera. It's ideal for projects where you don't plan to do much editing—think event coverage, quick turnaround videos, or behind-the-scenes clips. The Standard profile delivers a polished look without requiring post-production tweaks.

Neutral

Neutral reduces contrast and saturation slightly, preserving more detail in shadows and highlights. It's a great choice when you want a softer, more natural image or when you plan to make minor adjustments in editing without committing to a full color grade. Neutral can be especially flattering for interviews or moody, low-contrast scenes.

Canon Log 3 (C-Log 3)

This is the professional-grade option for maximum flexibility in post-production. C-Log 3 captures a much wider dynamic range, keeping highlight and shadow detail that Standard or Neutral might lose. The image will look flat and desaturated in-camera—this is intentional. You'll apply color correction and grading later to shape the final look.

Dynamic Range Optimization

Dynamic range is the ability to capture detail in both bright and dark areas of your scene. The R6 Mark II already has an impressive sensor, but your choice of profile affects how much of that range is preserved.

- **Standard** compresses highlights and shadows slightly to produce a punchy, ready-to-watch image.

- **Neutral** maintains a more balanced exposure curve, offering a bit more room for adjustment.

- **C-Log 3** keeps the most highlight and shadow detail, giving you freedom to adjust exposure in editing without introducing noise or banding.

Pro Tip: When shooting high-contrast scenes—like a bride stepping from bright sunlight into a shaded doorway—C-Log 3 will preserve more detail for post.

Shooting Flat for Color Grading in Post

If you choose to shoot in C-Log 3, your footage will look dull and washed out at first. That's the point—flat footage gives you more control later.

When shooting flat:

- **Expose carefully**: Slightly overexposing by half a stop can help keep noise out of shadow areas, but avoid blowing out highlights.
- **Monitor with a LUT**: You can apply a temporary LUT to your camera's display so you can see a more "finished" image while recording, even though the file remains flat.

Recommended LUTs for Quick Editing

A LUT (Look-Up Table) is like a preset for your video—it transforms the flat footage into a more stylized or natural look instantly.

For Canon R6 Mark II C-Log 3 footage, consider:

- **Canon's Official C-Log 3 to Rec.709 LUT**: Perfect for a true-to-life base color grade.

- **CineStyle LUTs**: Give your footage a film-like warmth and richness.

- **Neutral Film LUTs**: Maintain natural skin tones while adding cinematic depth.

- **Custom LUTs for Projects**: If you're building a consistent brand look, creating your own LUTs ensures uniform style across videos.

Pro Tip: Apply a base LUT to get your footage into a workable color space, then fine-tune contrast, saturation, and individual color channels for the final polish.

Bringing It All Together

If you want speed, Standard is your friend—what you see is what you get. If you want subtle flexibility, Neutral lets you tweak without a full grade. But if you're chasing cinematic quality and have time in post, C-Log 3 is the ultimate choice. Pair it with the right LUTs and grading workflow, and the R6 Mark II becomes a powerful cinematic tool that can match far more expensive cinema cameras.

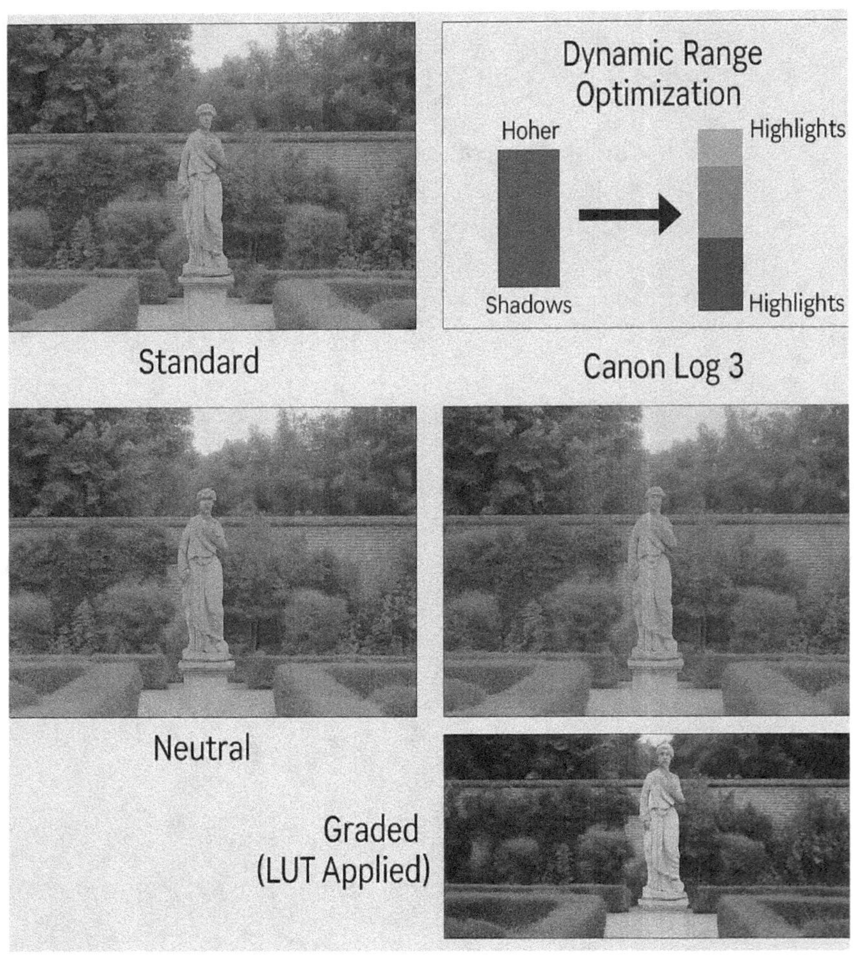

Chapter 12

Audio Capture for Film & Content Creation

Good visuals can grab attention, but it's great audio that keeps people engaged. Viewers might tolerate a slightly imperfect image, but poor sound will make them click away in seconds. The Canon EOS R6 Mark II is capable of producing professional-grade audio—if you know how to capture it well. This chapter walks you through everything from choosing the right microphone to controlling sound in challenging environments.

Built-in Mic vs. External Mics

The R6 Mark II includes a built-in stereo microphone—handy for casual filming, behind-the-scenes clips, or reference audio during shoots. However, built-in mics have limitations:

- They pick up camera handling noise.

- They capture more ambient sound than desired.

- They lack the depth and directionality of professional mics.

External microphones are the industry standard for serious filmmaking or content creation. The most common options are:

Shotgun Microphones

Highly directional, these mics focus on what's in front of them and reject sound from the sides and rear. Perfect for interviews, vlogs, and capturing dialogue in controlled setups. Mount them on your camera's hot shoe or use a boom pole for even cleaner sound.

Lavalier Microphones (Lavs)

Small, clip-on mics that attach to clothing, perfect for discreetly capturing clear speech. They're ideal for interviews, presentations, or YouTube tutorials. Wired lavs plug directly into the camera, while wireless lav systems give talent complete mobility.

Pro Tip: If you can, use an external recorder like a Zoom H5 or Tascam DR-10L for lavs. You'll capture higher-quality audio and have a backup track in case of camera recording issues.

Adjusting Audio Levels In-Camera

Clean audio starts with correct gain settings. On the R6 Mark II:

1. Plug in your external mic and switch the camera to Movie Mode.

2. Open the Sound Recording menu.

3. Switch from "Auto" to "Manual" for full control.

4. Set levels so your loudest sounds peak just below the red clipping zone—around -12dB on the meter.

Avoiding Clipping: If levels hit the red consistently, the audio will distort beyond repair. Always leave headroom for unexpected volume spikes.

Monitoring with Headphones

One of the most overlooked steps in video production is live audio monitoring. The R6 Mark II has a headphone jack—use it. Wearing headphones allows you to:

- Catch background hums, buzzes, or interference before they ruin a take.

- Hear if a mic cable is loose or crackling.

- Notice wind noise or clothing rustle from lavs.

Tip for Solo Filmmakers: Even if you can't wear headphones during the entire shoot, test your audio in a quick rehearsal to catch issues before recording a long take.

Reducing Background Noise On Set

Even the best microphone will pick up unwanted sound if the environment isn't controlled. Here's how to tame it:

- **Choose the Quietest Location Possible**

  Turn off fans, air conditioners, and refrigerators if they're within earshot. Close windows to block traffic or outdoor noise.

- **Use Directional Mics & Wind Protection**

  Outdoors, always use a deadcat (furry windscreen) on shotgun mics. Indoors, a foam windscreen can reduce plosives from speech.

- **Control Echo**

  Bare walls and hard floors create reverb. Add blankets, curtains, or foam panels to dampen sound reflections.

- **Mic Placement Matters**

  Keep microphones close to the source—within 6–12 inches for lavs, and just out of frame for shotguns.

Final Thoughts

Audio is half the story, and the R6 Mark II gives you the tools to get it right. Whether you're recording an intimate interview, a bustling city scene, or a YouTube tutorial, pairing the right mic with the right settings can make your content sound as good as it looks. Never underestimate the value of monitoring, adjusting levels manually, and controlling your environment.

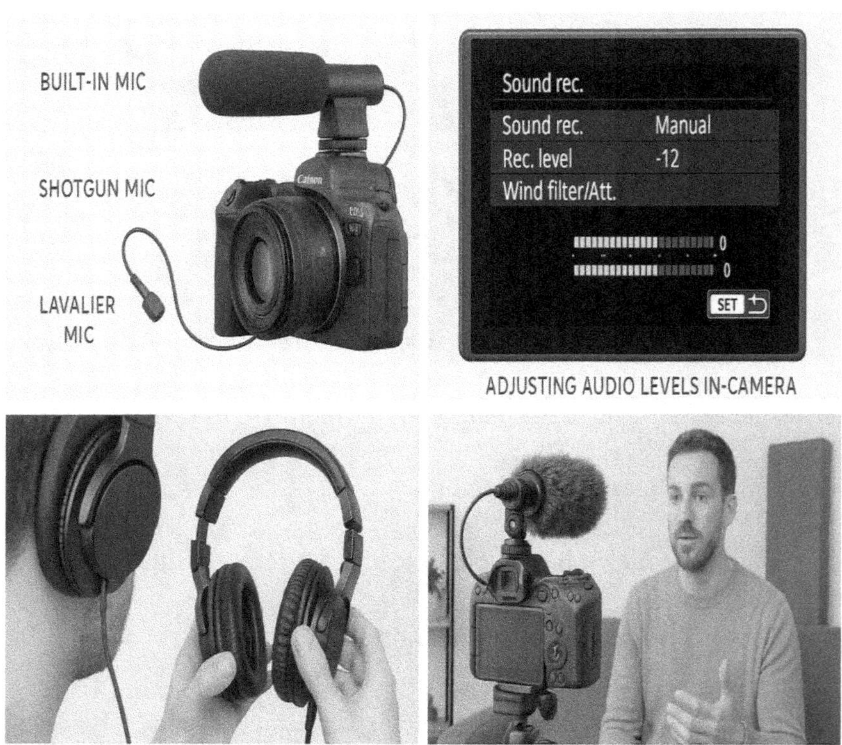

ADJUSTING AUDIO LEVELS IN-CAMERA

MONITORING WITH HEADPHONES

REDUCING BACKGROUND NOISE ON SET

Chapter 13

Stabilization for Handheld Shooting

Shaky footage can ruin an otherwise beautifully shot scene. The Canon EOS R6 Mark II was designed with a powerful stabilization system to give your handheld shots a smooth, professional look—whether you're filming a cinematic walking scene, a dynamic action sequence, or capturing stills in low light without a tripod. This chapter will help you master the different stabilization options and techniques so you can work confidently in any shooting situation.

In-Body IS and Digital IS

One of the standout features of the R6 Mark II is In-Body Image Stabilization (IBIS). This system physically shifts the camera's sensor to counteract hand movements, letting you shoot at slower shutter speeds or film without jitter.

- **IBIS Strengths:** Excellent for still photography and handheld video, especially when paired with wide-to-mid focal lengths.

- **Digital IS:** This is an additional layer of stabilization applied electronically during video recording. It crops slightly into the frame but adds an extra level of smoothness for handheld footage.

Tip: For general handheld video, use IBIS + Digital IS together, but be aware that excessive cropping can slightly reduce your field of view.

Combining Lens Stabilization with IBIS

Many RF and EF lenses have Optical Image Stabilization (OIS) built in. When used with the R6 Mark II's IBIS, you get coordinated stabilization, which can achieve up to 7–8 stops of correction.

- **Wide Lenses:** The stabilization works exceptionally well—handheld shots can look like they were taken on a tripod.

- **Telephoto Lenses:** The combination of OIS and IBIS is a lifesaver, as telephotos amplify every tiny shake.

Pro Tip: Make sure both the lens switch and the in-camera stabilization setting are turned on for them to work in harmony.

Gimbal Setups for Smooth Cinematic Footage

While IBIS and lens stabilization do wonders, a motorized gimbal is still the gold standard for ultra-smooth cinematic motion. Popular models like the DJI RS 3 or Zhiyun Weebill S can carry the R6 Mark II comfortably.

- **Balancing is Key:** Spend the time to balance your camera properly on the gimbal to avoid motor strain.
- **Modes to Explore:** Use "Follow Mode" for walking shots, "Lock Mode" for stable pans, and "POV Mode" for creative tilts and spins.

- **Pair with IBIS:** When shooting with a gimbal, you can keep IBIS on for subtle corrections, but avoid excessive Digital IS to prevent unnatural motion artifacts.

Tripod & Monopod Shooting Techniques

Sometimes, the simplest stabilization method is the most effective. A tripod or monopod is still an essential tool for any serious photographer or filmmaker.

- **Tripod Advantages:** Perfect for interviews, landscapes, and static shots where absolute stability is needed. Use a fluid head for smooth panning.
- **Monopod Versatility:** Great for sports, events, or situations where you need mobility but still want support.
- **Extra Tip:** Even on a tripod, turn off IBIS for completely static shots to prevent the system from "hunting" for movement that isn't there.

Final Thoughts

The R6 Mark II's stabilization technology gives you freedom to create without constantly worrying about shake. Whether you're shooting handheld in a fast-moving scene, filming a slow cinematic walk, or locking down your camera for a professional interview, mastering these stabilization methods will dramatically improve the quality of your work. Smooth, steady footage isn't just a technical choice—it's a storytelling choice that keeps your audience focused on your message, not your camera movement.

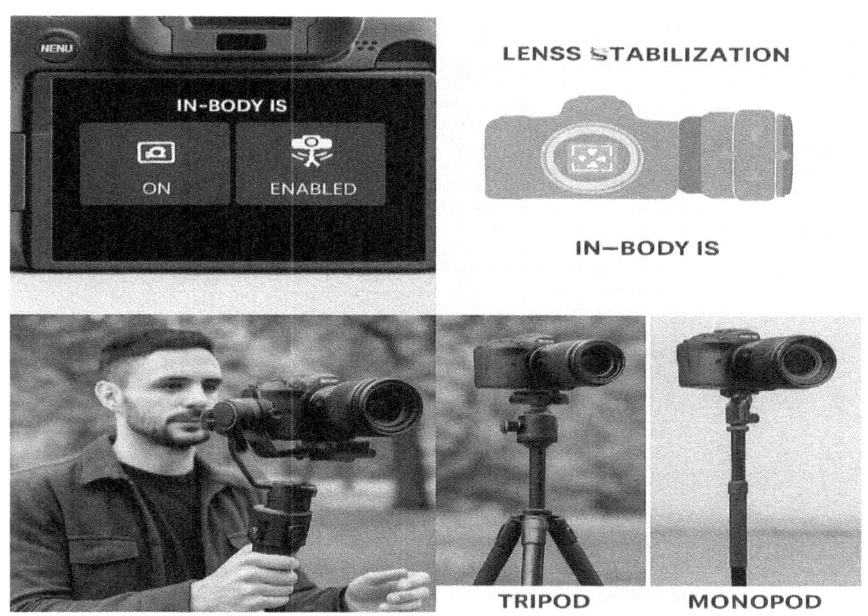

Chapter 14

Real-Life Filmmaking Scenarios

One of the greatest strengths of the Canon EOS R6 Mark II is its ability to adapt to a wide range of real-world filmmaking needs. Whether you're producing a daily vlog, filming a once-in-a-lifetime wedding, conducting a thoughtful documentary interview, or crafting a short cinematic piece, this camera offers the flexibility and performance to make each project shine. In this chapter, we'll break down specific setups, workflows, and techniques for four common scenarios.

Vlogging & YouTube Setups

If you're creating content for YouTube or social media, the R6 Mark II's fully articulating screen and reliable autofocus make it a dream companion.

- **Essential Setup:** Pair the camera with a compact wide-angle lens (like the RF 16mm f/2.8) for a flattering, immersive frame.

- **Audio:** Use a shotgun microphone mounted on the hot shoe for crisp dialogue, or a wireless lav mic for movement-heavy segments.

- **Settings for Success:** Record at 4K 30p for standard content or 4K 60p for smoother motion. Enable Face + Eye AF to keep yourself sharp even if you move around.

- **Lighting:** Keep a small LED light handy for consistent illumination indoors or during low light.

Pro Tip: Pre-program your settings into a custom shooting mode (C1 or C2) so you can start recording instantly without fumbling through menus.

Wedding Videography Workflow

Wedding shoots demand adaptability, speed, and reliability—qualities the R6 Mark II delivers in spades.

- **Two-Body Setup:** Use one camera with a fast prime lens (e.g., 50mm f/1.2) for intimate shots and another with a zoom (24–70mm f/2.8) for versatility.

- **Stabilization:** For ceremony and speeches, use a tripod or monopod. For dynamic moments like the first dance, switch to a gimbal for fluid motion.

- **Settings:** 4K oversampled footage from the R6 Mark II offers stunning detail. Shoot at 24p for a cinematic feel and use dual card recording for redundancy.

- **Audio:** Capture clean sound with both an on-camera mic and a dedicated audio recorder connected to the venue's sound system.

Pro Tip: Use C-Log 3 for maximum dynamic range to handle bright outdoor ceremonies and dimly lit receptions without losing detail.

Documentary & Interview Setups

Documentaries and interviews require a setup that's unobtrusive yet capable of delivering professional image and audio quality.

- **Lens Choice:** A 35mm or 50mm prime keeps a natural perspective without distortion.

- **Lighting:** A softbox or LED panel placed at a 45-degree angle provides flattering, soft light.

- **Settings:** 4K 24p or 30p is ideal. Keep shutter speed at double the frame rate (e.g., 1/50 for 24p) for natural motion.

- **Audio:** Use a lavalier mic for the subject and monitor audio levels through headphones. Always record a backup track.

Pro Tip: Lock in white balance manually to avoid color shifts mid-interview.

Short Film Production Tips

Short films allow you to push the R6 Mark II's creative limits, from dynamic camera movement to precise color grading.

- **Planning:** Storyboard your shots and plan lens choices ahead of time.

- **Cinematic Look:** Shoot at 24p, use ND filters for outdoor daylight scenes, and frame with intentional composition.

- **Movement:** Mix handheld shots for intimacy with gimbal shots for polish.

- **Post-Production Workflow:** Record in C-Log 3 for flexibility in grading, and use LUTs as a starting point before fine-tuning color.

Pro Tip: Use focus peaking during rehearsals to nail focus in shallow depth-of-field shots.

Final Thoughts

The Canon EOS R6 Mark II isn't just a camera—it's a creative partner that can handle the unpredictable demands of real-life filmmaking. By customizing your settings, choosing the right accessories, and adapting your approach for each scenario, you can ensure that your final product not only meets professional standards but also resonates deeply with your audience.

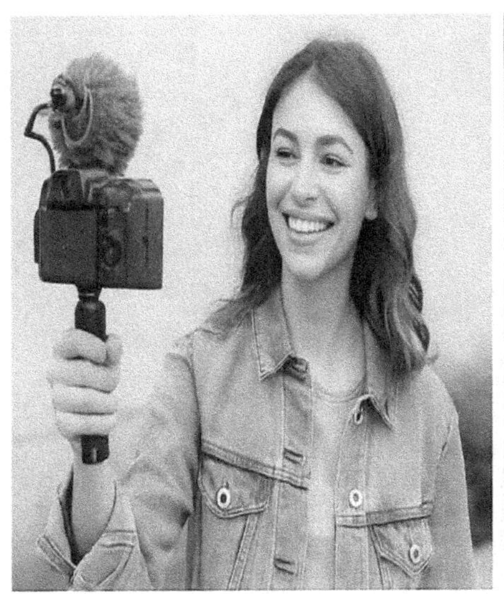

Vlogging & YouTube Setups

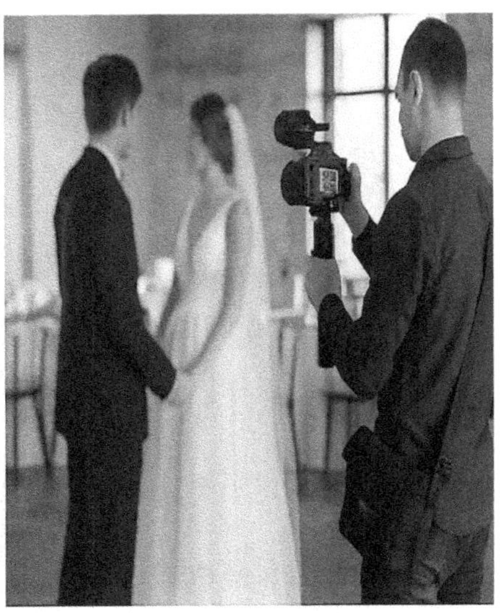

Wedding Videography
Workflow

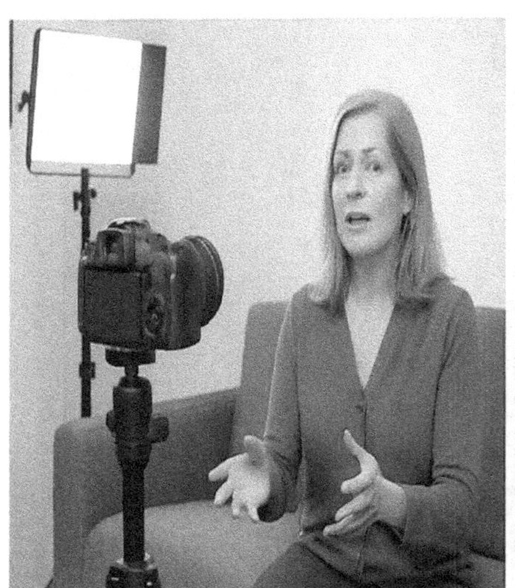

Documentary/Interview
Setups

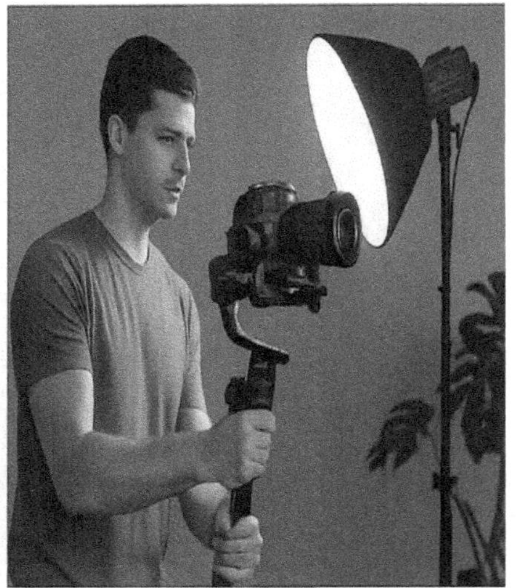

Short Film
Production Tips

Chapter 15

Lenses & Accessories That Unlock Potential

The Canon EOS R6 Mark II is a powerhouse of a camera, but its true potential is only unlocked when paired with the right lenses and accessories. Whether you're a stills photographer, a dedicated filmmaker, or someone who moves fluidly between the two, your choice of gear directly shapes your results. This chapter is about equipping you not only with the right tools but also with the reasoning behind each choice, so every lens or accessory you invest in has a clear purpose in your creative workflow.

Best Prime and Zoom Lenses for Stills

1. Prime Lenses – Crisp, Fast, and Full of Character

Prime lenses are fixed focal length lenses—no zoom capability—

but they often deliver sharper results, wider apertures, and better low-light performance than their zoom counterparts.

- **Canon RF 50mm f/1.8 STM** – The affordable "nifty fifty" for portraits, street photography, and general use. It's lightweight, discreet, and produces beautiful background blur (bokeh).

- **Canon RF 35mm f/1.8 Macro IS STM** – Great for environmental portraits, food photography, and detail shots. The macro capability adds versatility for product or close-up work.

- **Canon RF 85mm f/2 Macro IS STM** – A flattering portrait lens with creamy bokeh and macro capability for fine detail work, perfect for weddings or close-up storytelling.

Why primes matter: They force you to move your feet, think about framing, and work with more intentionality. The wide maximum apertures (f/1.2, f/1.4, f/1.8) allow for stunning shallow depth-of-field and improved low-light shooting.

2. Zoom Lenses – Flexibility in a Single Lens

Zooms allow you to adapt to different focal lengths without changing lenses—a huge advantage in fast-paced shooting situations.

- **Canon RF 24-70mm f/2.8L IS USM** – The workhorse lens for events, weddings, and everyday coverage. Sharp, fast, and perfect for both portraits and landscapes.

- **Canon RF 70-200mm f/2.8L IS USM** – Ideal for sports, wildlife, and candid portraits from a distance. Offers creamy bokeh at longer focal lengths.

- **Canon RF 24-105mm f/4L IS USM** – A versatile all-in-one travel lens that balances performance, reach, and portability.

Essential Video Lenses

When it comes to filmmaking, you want lenses that handle motion gracefully, offer smooth focus transitions, and provide cinematic rendering.

1. Wide Lenses for Establishing Shots

- **Canon RF 15-35mm f/2.8L IS USM** – Ultra-wide for landscapes, architecture, and immersive establishing shots in video.

- **Laowa 15mm f/2 Zero-D** – A specialty wide-angle with minimal distortion, excellent for real estate tours or stylized video work.

2. Fast Primes for Cinematic Depth

- **Canon RF 35mm f/1.8** – Lightweight, intimate feel, great for storytelling sequences.

- **Canon RF 50mm f/1.2L USM** – Stunning bokeh and light-gathering ability for dramatic close-ups and interviews.

3. Parfocal Zooms for Smooth Framing Changes

Parfocal lenses maintain focus while zooming—a crucial trait for video. While most stills lenses are not parfocal, certain cine lenses like the Canon CN-E zooms or Sigma Cine Zooms offer this ability for professional film setups.

Filters – Small Glass, Big Difference

Filters are not just for "effect"—they're essential tools for controlling light and protecting your investment.

- **UV Filters** – Primarily for lens protection. High-quality UV glass prevents scratches, dust, and moisture from damaging the front element.

- **Circular Polarizers (CPL)** – Cut glare and reflections in water or glass, deepen skies, and enrich colors.

- **Neutral Density (ND) Filters** – Reduce light without affecting color, essential for shooting at cinematic shutter speeds in bright conditions. Variable NDs are perfect for run-and-gun video.

Extra Batteries & Storage Solutions

The EOS R6 Mark II is power-hungry, especially when shooting 4K or using the electronic viewfinder extensively.

1. Batteries

- **Canon LP-E6NH** – The official high-capacity battery for maximum shooting time.
- Carry at least 2–3 spares for all-day events or travel.

2. Memory Cards

- **UHS-II SD Cards** – Recommended for high-bitrate 4K and burst photography. Look for cards with a **V90** rating for the fastest sustained speeds.
- Have multiple cards to swap quickly between shoots and avoid the risk of losing all your work in one card failure.

3. Backup Storage

- Portable SSDs like the Samsung T7 Shield for field backups.

- Cloud backup integration for instant upload if working on location with Wi-Fi.

Why This Matters

The right lens or accessory doesn't just add to your gear—it shapes your creative possibilities. A good lens lets the EOS R6 Mark II truly shine, capturing more detail, depth, and dynamic range. Proper accessories ensure you can work faster, protect your investment, and produce higher-quality results in any scenario.

Best Prime and Zoom Lenses for Stills

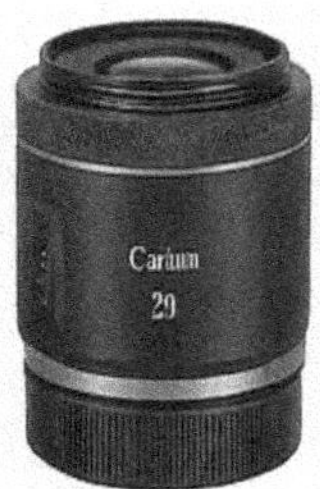 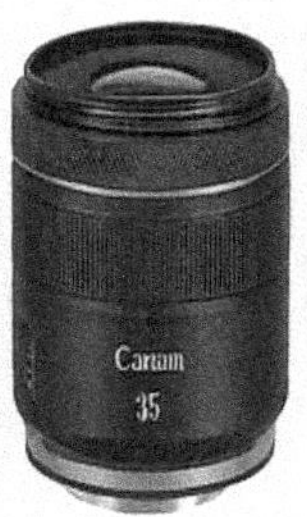 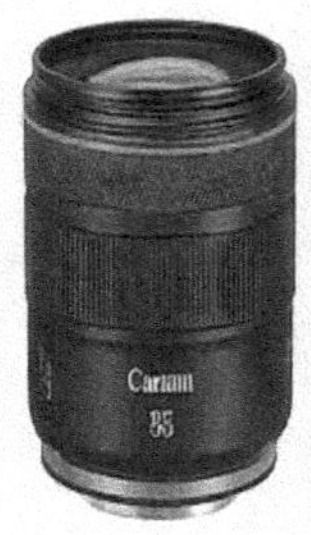 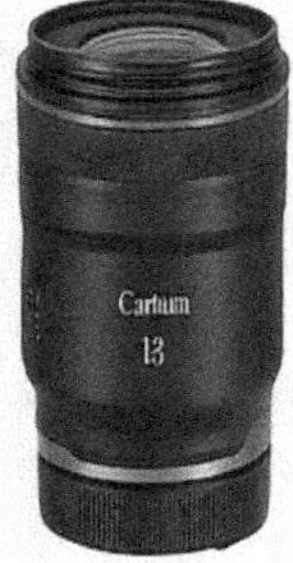

Canon RF
15 mm f/ 2,6 L

Canon RF 18
Macro IS STM

Canon RF
35 mm f/1,8

Laowa 15mm
f/2 Zero-D

Essential Video Lenses

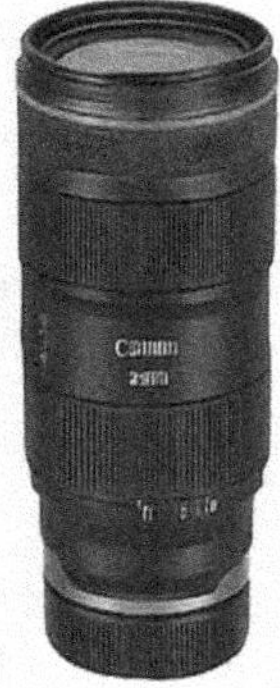 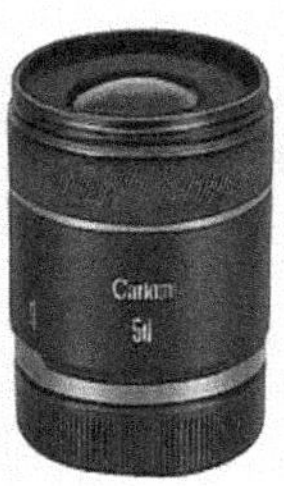 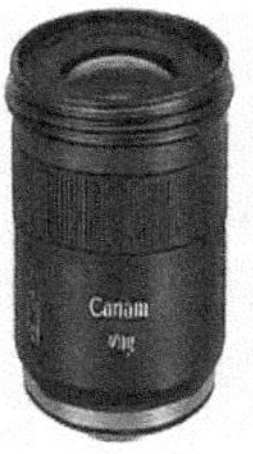 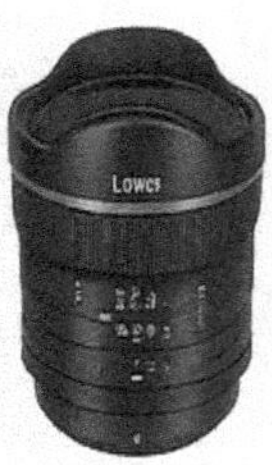

Canon RF
15-35mm f/2 L

Canon RF 1,8

35mm

Laowa 5,z
Zero-D

Filters, Extra Batteries, and Storage Solutions

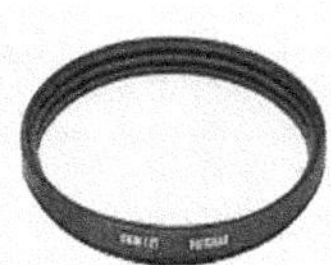 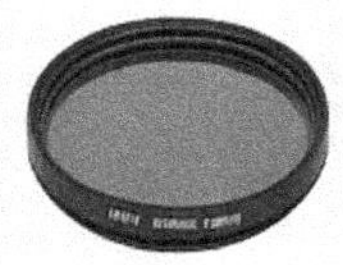 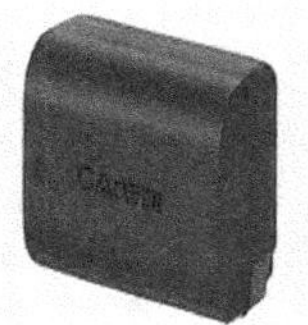 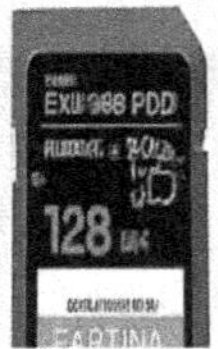

Chapter 16

Editing Workflow for Photographers & Filmmakers

When you've captured the perfect moment—or an entire day's worth of footage—the creative process doesn't end with pressing the shutter or stopping the record button. In many ways, that's just the first half of the story. The editing stage is where you shape raw material into a polished, intentional final product that resonates with your audience. For both photographers and filmmakers, having a clear, efficient workflow is the bridge between capturing great content and presenting it in its best possible form.

Importing and Organizing in Lightroom &

Premiere Pro

The first step to a professional editing process is file management. Chaos at this stage will cost you hours later.

1. Transferring Your Files

- Use a high-speed card reader to transfer files from your memory cards rather than connecting your camera directly. This reduces wear on the camera ports and speeds up transfer times.
- Immediately create a backup—either on an external drive or a cloud service—before you start working. Memory cards can fail, and nothing hurts more than losing irreplaceable shots.

2. Organizing for Photography (Lightroom Classic)

- **Create a clear folder structure** by shoot date and project name:

  2025-03-15 – Engagement Shoot – Smith & Davis

- In Lightroom, use the Import Dialog to add keywords, metadata, and copyright information during import. This saves you time later and ensures every image is tagged.

- Apply a basic metadata preset to include your name and copyright info on every file automatically.

3. Organizing for Video (Adobe Premiere Pro)

- Create a project folder that contains subfolders for:

  o Footage

  o Audio

  o Graphics

  o Exports

- Inside Premiere, import files into Bins that match this structure. Organizing bins by shoot day, camera angle, or scene makes the editing process intuitive and fast.

Basic Color Correction and Grading

Both still images and video benefit from adjustments that correct color and enhance mood.

1. Color Correction

- **Photography:** In Lightroom, start with the Basic Panel—adjust white balance, exposure, contrast, and shadows/highlights to correct for natural variances in lighting.

- **Video:** In Premiere Pro, use the Lumetri Color Panel. Start with the *Basic Correction* tab to ensure your footage is balanced and neutral before adding creative touches.

2. Color Grading

- This is where your creative intent takes the lead. For portraits, you might warm the tones to enhance skin texture. For landscapes, you may push blues and greens for vibrancy.

- For video, consider using Canon Log 3 (C-Log 3) footage if you shot in that profile—it provides a wide dynamic range and flexibility in grading. Apply a LUT (Look-Up Table) to quickly give your footage a polished starting point, then tweak from there.

3. Consistency Across Clips and Photos

- Apply global adjustments to maintain a consistent look and feel. This is crucial for multi-clip videos or a series of images meant to be displayed together.

Export Settings for Social Media, Web, and Print

The final step—exporting—should be driven by how and where your work will be viewed.

1. For Social Media

- **Photos:** Export JPEGs at 2048 pixels on the long edge, sRGB color space, and 80–90% quality for sharpness without heavy file sizes.

- **Videos:** Export in H.264 format, 1080p or 4K, depending on platform requirements. Keep bitrate around 10–20 Mbps for online viewing without excessive compression artifacts.

2. For Web Use

- Match your platform's recommended resolutions. For blogs or portfolios, a 3000px long edge photo ensures clarity. For video, 4K exports future-proof your content.

- Always embed an sRGB profile for web display to ensure colors appear accurately across devices.

3. For Print

- **Photos:** Export TIFF or high-quality JPEGs at 300 DPI, in Adobe RGB or ProPhoto RGB for wider color gamut printing.

- Work with your print lab's specifications—they may request a particular format or size.

- **Videos:** If delivering to a festival or client, check their preferred codec and resolution, such as ProRes 422 HQ or DNxHD for master files.

Pro Tips for a Smoother Workflow

- **Name your files intelligently**: Instead of `IMG_0302.CR3`, rename to `R6MkII_Portrait_Day1_001.CR3`—it makes searching and sorting infinitely easier.

- **Work from a copy**, not your original card or archive, to avoid accidental overwrites.

- **Batch process** where possible—sync adjustments in Lightroom, or use adjustment layers in Premiere.

- Keep color-calibrated monitors for accurate viewing; your final product will look consistent across devices and prints.

Closing Thought:

Editing is not about "fixing" mistakes—it's about refining and amplifying your creative vision. Whether you're polishing a wedding highlight reel or preparing a photo spread for a client, the R6 Mark II's high-quality files give you the flexibility to push your edits without breaking image quality. Master this workflow, and your audience will notice not just the technical clarity of your work, but the professional consistency that keeps them coming back for more.

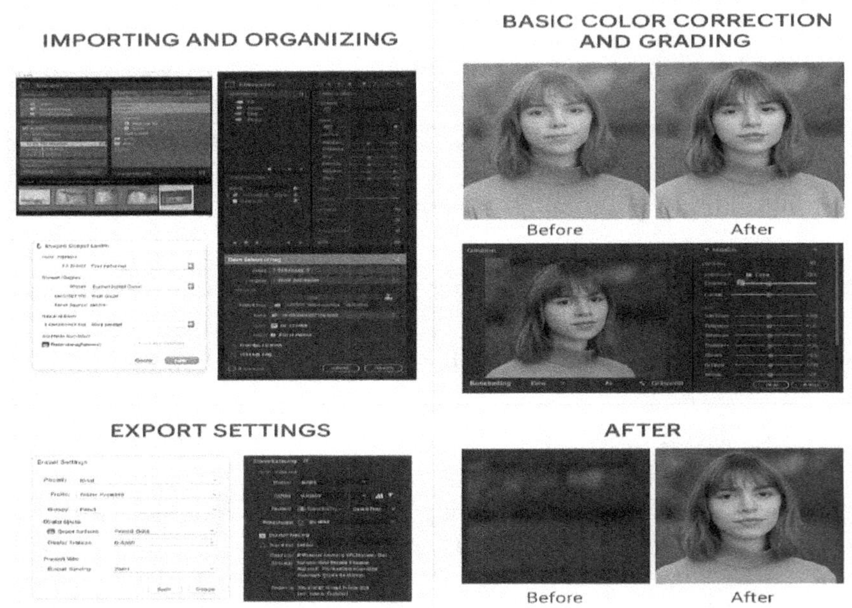

Part V: Quick Reference & Troubleshooting

Chapter 17

Quick Settings Cheat Sheets

When you're in the middle of a shoot, the last thing you want is to fumble through menus trying to remember the perfect combination of settings. A good photographer anticipates the conditions and has their camera ready before the moment unfolds. The Canon EOS R6 Mark II gives you incredible flexibility, but that also means endless choices — and without a clear starting point, it's easy to get lost. This chapter is your "ready-to-go" settings guide, designed to give you practical, field-tested setups for the four most common scenarios: portraits, sports, landscapes, and video.

Portrait Photography Settings

Portraits are about capturing personality, emotion, and flattering light. Whether you're photographing a loved one in the backyard or a client in a studio, you want a shallow depth of field, pleasing skin tones, and sharp eyes.

- **Mode:** Aperture Priority (Av) — lets you control depth of field while the camera handles shutter speed.

- **Aperture:** f/1.8 to f/2.8 with prime lenses, f/4 on zooms — creates background blur while keeping the subject sharp.

- **ISO:** Auto ISO with max limit around 3200 for low-light flexibility.

- **AF Method:** Face + Eye Detection AF enabled.

- **Drive Mode:** Single shot for posed portraits, continuous low speed for candid moments.

- **White Balance:** Daylight for outdoor shoots, Auto or Custom for mixed lighting.

- **Picture Style:** Portrait — softens skin tones while preserving detail.

Pro Tip: Position your subject away from the background and shoot with longer focal lengths (85mm or higher) for maximum background compression and creamy bokeh.

Sports & Action Photography Settings

For fast-moving subjects, you need speed, precision, and reliability in your focusing system. The R6 Mark II's advanced autofocus tracking can lock onto athletes, wildlife, or even fast-moving kids with ease.

- **Mode:** Shutter Priority (Tv) or Manual with Auto ISO.
- **Shutter Speed:** 1/1000s minimum for sports, 1/2000s for extremely fast action like motorsports.
- **Aperture:** Wide open (f/2.8–f/4) for isolating the subject.
- **ISO:** Auto with max limit around 6400.
- **AF Method:** Tracking: Spot AF or Zone AF depending on subject size. Enable Eye/Animal AF if needed.
- **Drive Mode:** High-Speed Continuous (H+).

- **White Balance:** Auto or custom if shooting under stadium lights.

- **Picture Style:** Standard or Neutral for maximum flexibility in post.

Pro Tip: Pre-focus on an area where the action will happen and follow through the motion — the R6 Mark II will keep tracking the subject as it moves.

Landscape Photography Settings

Landscapes require detail from foreground to horizon, accurate color, and minimal noise. You'll often work at smaller apertures for deep focus and use a tripod when possible.

- **Mode:** Aperture Priority (Av) for control over depth of field.

- **Aperture:** f/8 to f/11 for maximum sharpness.

- **ISO:** Keep at 100 for the cleanest image quality.

- **Shutter Speed:** Will vary — use a tripod if slower than 1/60s.

- **AF Method:** One Shot AF, focus one-third into the frame for optimal depth.

- **Drive Mode:** Single shot.

- **White Balance:** Daylight or set manually for golden hour warmth.

- **Picture Style:** Landscape — boosts blues and greens for vibrant outdoor scenes.

Pro Tip: Enable the grid lines in the viewfinder to maintain level horizons, and use exposure bracketing if shooting high-contrast scenes.

Video Shooting Settings

Video is where the R6 Mark II truly shines, offering professional-quality footage in a compact body. The goal is to balance smooth motion, accurate exposure, and clean audio.

- **Mode:** Manual (M) for full control.

- **Resolution:** 4K UHD oversampled from 6K for maximum detail.

- **Frame Rate:**

    o 24p for cinematic look.

    o 60p for smooth motion or slow motion in post.

- **Shutter Speed:** Double your frame rate (e.g., 1/50s for 24p, 1/125s for 60p).

- **Aperture:** f/2.8–f/5.6 depending on depth of field desired.

- **ISO:** Keep as low as possible — raise only when needed.

- **AF Method:** Continuous AF with Face + Eye Detection enabled.

- **Picture Profile:** Canon Log 3 for maximum grading flexibility.

- **Audio:** External shotgun or lavalier mic plugged into 3.5mm jack, monitor via headphones.

Pro Tip: Use ND filters in bright light to keep your aperture wide without overexposing the scene.

By saving these settings to the R6 Mark II's custom shooting modes (C1, C2, C3 on the mode dial), you can switch between portrait, action, landscape, and video setups in seconds. This is one of the most powerful time-saving features for photographers and videographers who shoot a mix of genres.

PORTRATS

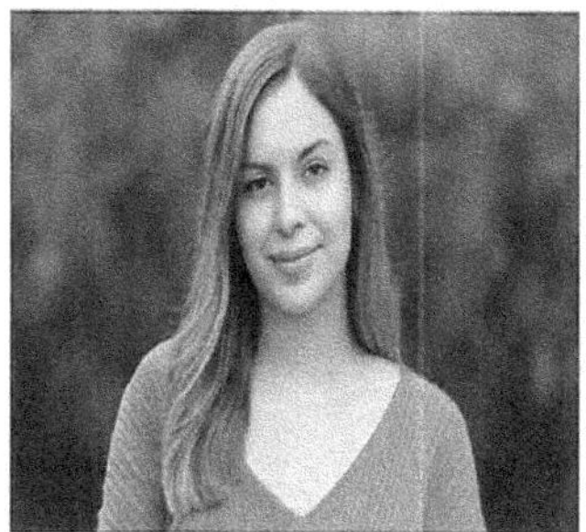

Best Settings: Av
Aperture: f/1.8–2.2.8
Auto ISO (Max 3200)"
Face + Eye AF ara enabled
Drive Mode: Single Shooting
White Balance: Daylight
Picture Style: Portrait

SPORTS

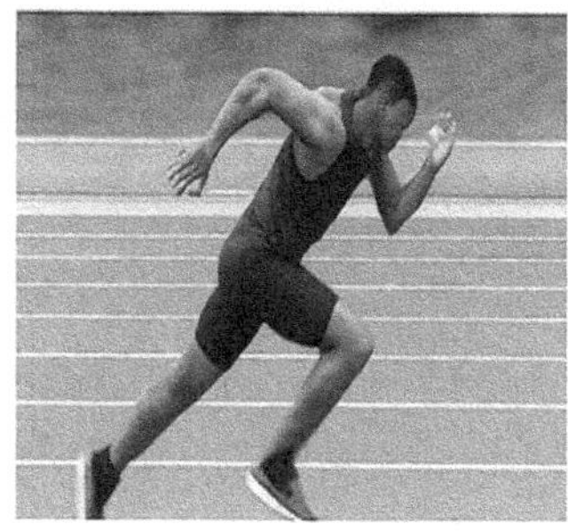

Best Settings: Ty or M
Shutter Speed: 1/1000s o faster
Aute ISO (Max 6400
Tracking: Spot AF
Drive Mode: High-Spf Continuous
White Balance: Auto
Picture Style: Standard or Neutral

LANDSCAPES

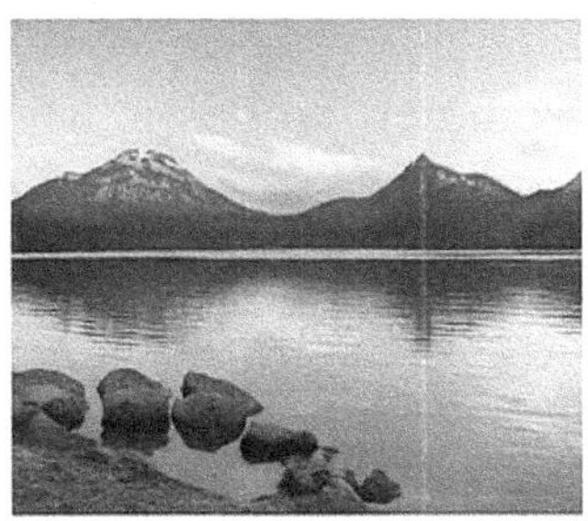

Best Settings: Av
Aperture: f/8–F11
ISO 100
One Shot AF

VIDEO

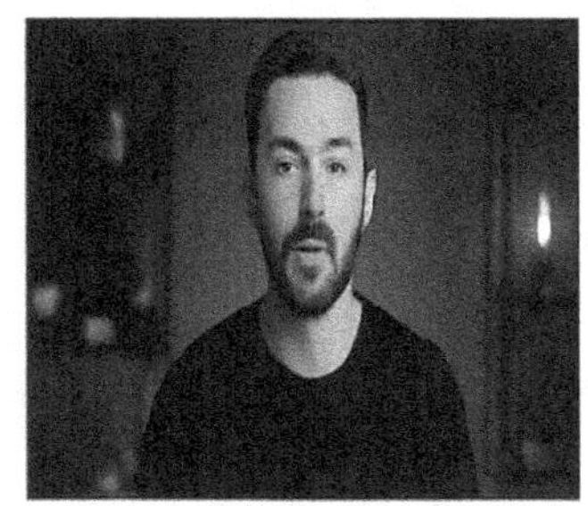

Best Settings: M
Resolution: 4K UHD
Frame Rate: 24p or 60p
Shutter Speed: 1/50 or 125

Chapter 18

Common Problems & How to Fix Them

Even the most advanced cameras, like the Canon EOS R6 Mark II, can run into hiccups—especially when you're in the middle of a shoot. Whether it's an unpredictable autofocus shift, a sudden blowout of highlights, or your camera overheating during an important video recording, knowing how to troubleshoot quickly can be the difference between saving the shot or losing it forever. This chapter focuses on the most common problems R6 Mark II users face and the practical, field-tested solutions to fix them on the spot.

1. Autofocus Hunting Solutions

Autofocus hunting is when your camera repeatedly searches for focus—usually shifting back and forth instead of locking onto your subject. This can be frustrating in both still photography and video, especially in low light or when shooting subjects with low contrast.

Possible Causes:

- Low-light conditions or lack of subject contrast.

- The AF mode isn't suited to the scene.

- Obstructions in the frame confusing the AF system (e.g., branches, moving objects).

Solutions:

- **Switch AF Method:** If using Face + Tracking, try switching to a single AF point or Zone AF to force the camera to focus where you want.

- **Increase Light or Contrast:** Adding a bit more light or aiming at a higher contrast area of your subject helps the camera lock focus faster.

- **Use Manual Override:** For tricky scenes, half-press the shutter to pre-focus, then switch to manual focus to lock it.

155

- **Update Firmware:** Canon often refines autofocus performance in firmware updates—keeping your camera updated ensures you benefit from those improvements.

2. Fixing Overexposure / Underexposure

Exposure issues—either too bright or too dark—can ruin an otherwise perfect shot. While the R6 Mark II's metering system is excellent, it can still be fooled by extreme lighting situations.

Signs of Overexposure: Washed-out highlights, lack of detail in bright areas.

Signs of Underexposure: Dark shadows with no recoverable detail.

Quick Fixes:

- **Use Exposure Compensation:** In semi-auto modes (Aperture Priority, Shutter Priority), dial in -1 to -2 stops for overexposure or +1 to +2 for underexposure.

- **Switch Metering Modes:** Evaluative metering works well for most scenes, but Spot or Partial metering is better when your subject is backlit or surrounded by very bright/dark areas.

- **Check Histogram:** Enable the histogram in your display and ensure your tonal range is not clipped on either end.

- **Shoot in RAW:** Even if you slightly miss exposure, RAW files allow for better recovery during post-processing compared to JPEGs.

3. Solving Overheating in Video Mode

Recording high-resolution 4K or oversampled 6K footage generates heat, especially in long takes. Overheating can trigger a shutdown warning, forcing you to stop filming.

Preventive Measures:

- **Lower Resolution or Frame Rate:** If you don't need 4K 60p or oversampled 6K, switch to 4K 30p or 1080p to reduce processing strain.

- **Enable High Frame Rate Mode Sparingly:** 120fps shooting is demanding—use it in short bursts.

- **Avoid Direct Sunlight:** Shade your camera or use a white cloth cover to prevent additional heat from the environment.

- **Take Cooling Breaks:** Plan your filming in segments with pauses to allow the camera to cool.

If Overheating Happens Mid-Shoot:

- Power off the camera and remove the battery for a few minutes.

- Use an external fan or cooling device if shooting in a controlled environment.

- Consider using an external recorder via HDMI—this can shift processing load away from the camera and reduce internal heat buildup.

By understanding these issues and how to respond, you'll be prepared to troubleshoot on the fly. A smooth shoot isn't just about knowing the R6 Mark II's features—it's also about staying calm, diagnosing problems quickly, and applying the right fix without

missing the moment.

Autofocus Hunting Solutions

When the camera has trouble locking onto subjects

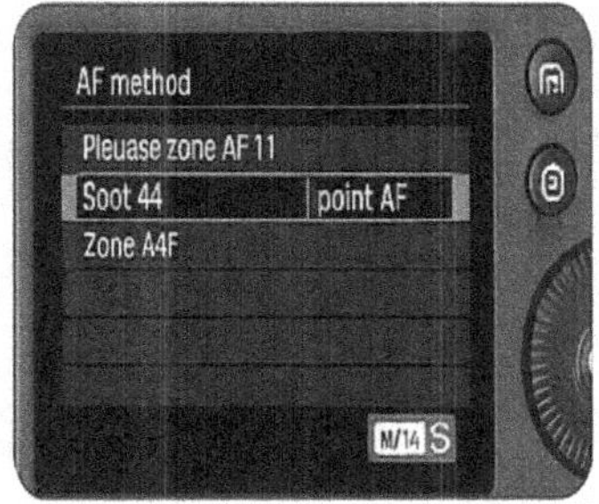

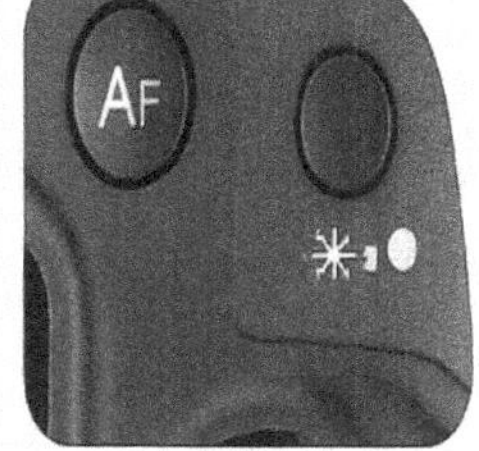

Use manual override

- Switch AF method
- Increase light or contrast

Fixing Overexposure/Underexposure

If images are too bright or too dark

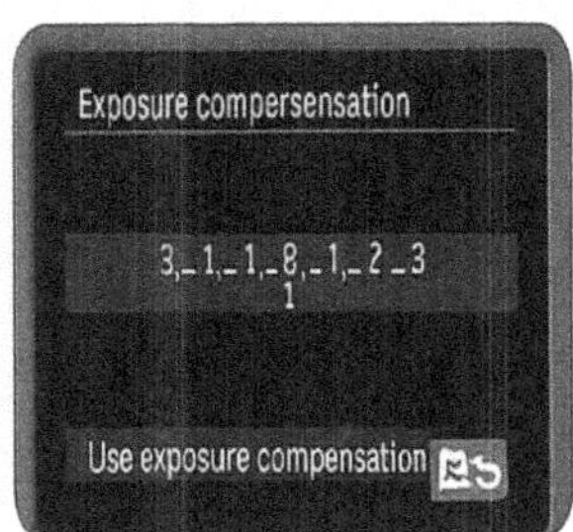

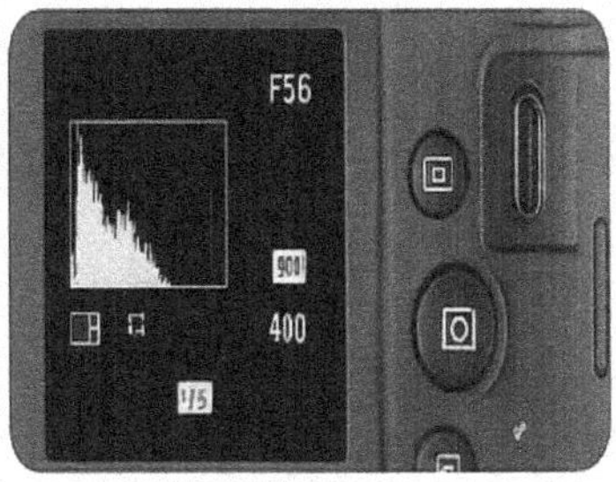

- Use exposure
  compensation

- Check histogram
- Switch metering mode

Chapter 19

Maintenance & Longevity Tips

Your Canon EOS R6 Mark II is more than just a tool—it's an investment in your craft. With the right care, it can serve you faithfully for years, delivering the same sharp, vibrant results as the day you first unboxed it. In this chapter, we'll focus on practical, real-world steps to keep your camera in peak condition, protect it from avoidable damage, and ensure it's always ready for action.

1. Cleaning the Sensor and Lenses

A clean sensor and lens aren't just about keeping dust spots off your images—they directly impact the sharpness, color accuracy, and overall quality of your shots.

Sensor Cleaning Basics:

- Use the camera's built-in sensor cleaning function before attempting any physical cleaning. This uses vibration to shake loose light dust.

- If stubborn specks remain, use a hand-squeezed air blower (never canned air, as it can spray propellant and damage the sensor).

- For visible smudges or stubborn debris, only attempt wet cleaning with a sensor swab if you are confident in the process; otherwise, have it professionally cleaned.

Lens Cleaning:

- Start with **a** soft lens brush or blower to remove loose particles.

- For fingerprints or smudges, use a microfiber cloth and lens cleaning solution, wiping in gentle circular motions from the center outward.

- Always keep a UV or clear protective filter on your lens to safeguard the front element.

2. Protecting Your Camera in Harsh Weather

Your R6 Mark II is weather-sealed, but "weather-sealed" doesn't mean indestructible. Long exposure to moisture, dust, or extreme temperatures can still cause problems.

In Rain or Snow:

- Use a dedicated rain cover or even a plastic bag in emergencies to shield your camera and lens.
- Avoid changing lenses in wet environments—moisture can enter the body quickly.

In Dusty or Sandy Areas:

- Keep your camera inside a zippered bag when not shooting.
- Avoid lens changes in open air.

In Extreme Cold:

- Keep batteries warm in your pocket; cold temperatures drain them faster.

- When returning indoors, seal the camera in a plastic bag until it reaches room temperature to prevent condensation.

In Heat:

- Store your gear out of direct sunlight.
- Use a light-colored camera cover to reflect heat during outdoor shoots.

3. Firmware Updates for New Features

Canon regularly releases firmware updates that not only fix bugs but often add new features and improve performance—especially for autofocus and video capabilities.

How to Update Firmware:

1. Visit the official Canon support page for the EOS R6 Mark II.
2. Download the latest firmware and copy it to a freshly formatted memory card.

3. Insert the card into the camera, go to the Setup menu, and select Firmware Update.

4. Follow the on-screen instructions carefully and ensure your battery is fully charged.

Why It Matters:

- Firmware updates can boost autofocus tracking, enhance video codecs, or even improve menu functionality.

- Some updates resolve known bugs that could save you from frustration in the field.

Final Thought

Your Canon EOS R6 Mark II will reward the care you give it. Keep it clean, shield it from environmental hazards, and keep the firmware fresh, and it will serve you faithfully—ready to capture every fleeting moment, from once-in-a-lifetime weddings to quiet sunsets in your backyard.

MAINTENANCE & LONGEVITY TIPS

CLEANING THE SENSOR AND LENSES

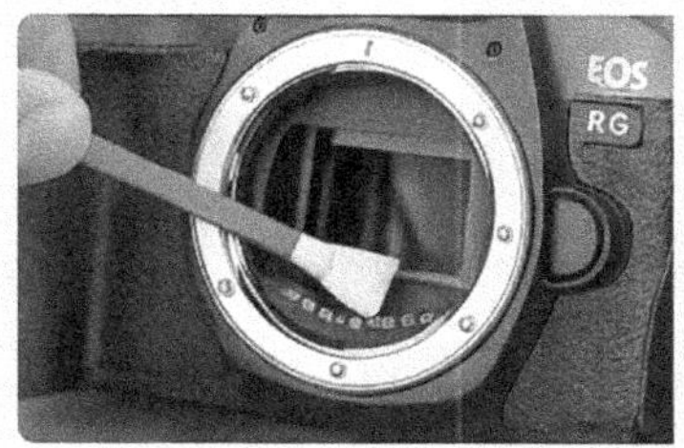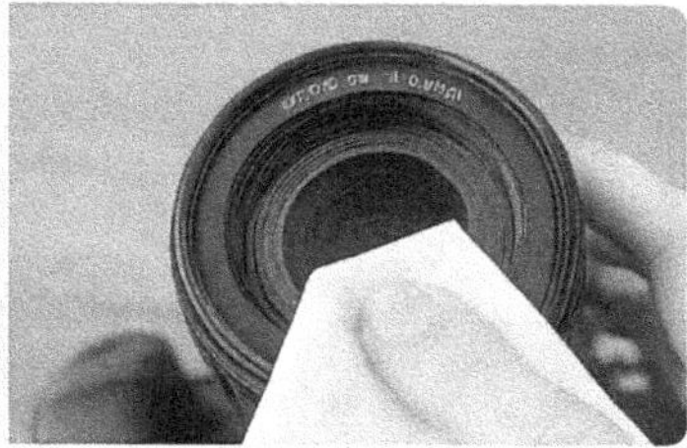

- Use a; hand-skeeesenoor cleàning secure pide
- Use a UV´cover clean with a marromatrovgifter'for a fulter

PROTECTING YOUR CAMERA IN HARSH WEATHER

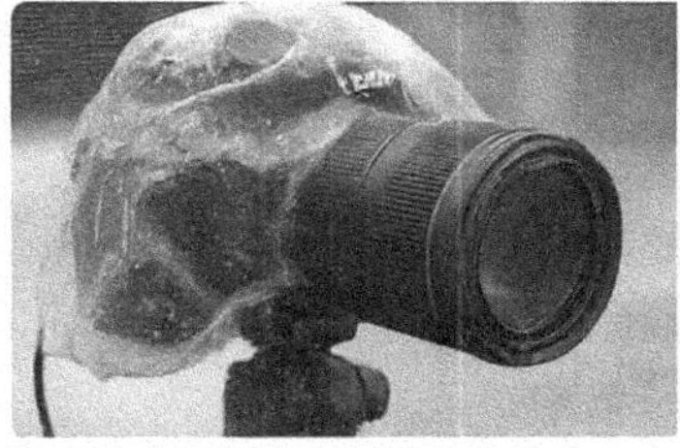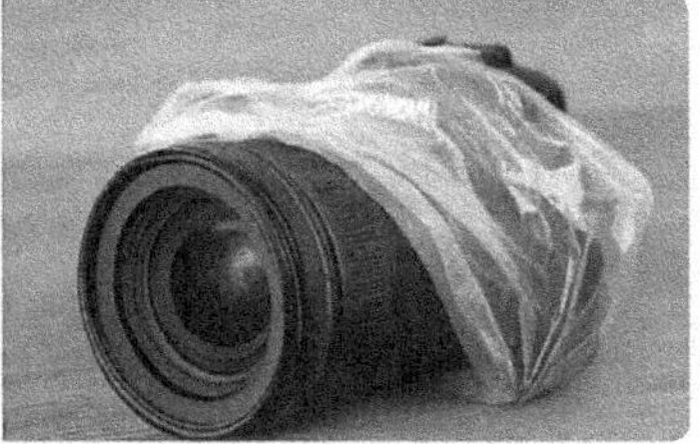

IN RAIN OR SNOW:
- Avoid protection protective for front cover

IN DUSTY OR SANDY AREAS:
- Avoid in a conidrous sensly area

FIRMWARE UPDATES FOR NEW FEATURES

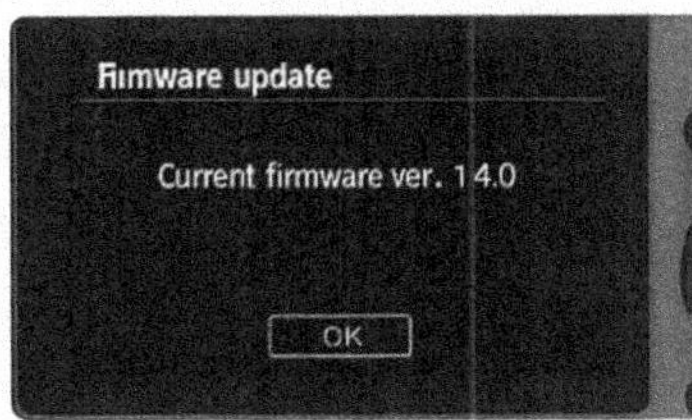

- Device official Canon sputo menu uptares
- Update firmwa re upgr ade

Cinematography Terms

Aperture – The adjustable opening inside a lens that controls the amount of light reaching the camera sensor. Measured in f-stops (e.g., f/2.8, f/5.6), with lower numbers letting in more light and creating shallower depth of field.

Bokeh – The pleasing blur in out-of-focus areas of an image, often used in portraits to isolate the subject.

Bitrate – The amount of data recorded per second of video. Higher bitrates often mean better quality but result in larger file sizes.

C-Log 3 – Canon's advanced flat color profile that captures a wide dynamic range for professional color grading in post-production.

Depth of Field (DoF) – The zone of sharp focus in an image. Controlled by aperture, focal length, and subject distance.

Dynamic Range – The camera sensor's ability to capture detail in both the darkest shadows and brightest highlights.

Frame Rate – The number of frames recorded per second in a video. Common examples: 24p (cinematic), 30p (web), 60p (smooth motion).

IBIS (In-Body Image Stabilization) – A camera feature that compensates for hand movement, allowing sharper photos and smoother handheld videos.

ISO – A setting that determines the camera sensor's sensitivity to light. Higher ISO helps in low light but increases noise.

Lens Mount – The physical connection between a lens and the camera body. The R6 Mark II uses Canon's RF mount.

Oversampling – Capturing video at a higher resolution (e.g., 6K) and then downscaling to 4K for sharper detail.

Shutter Speed – The amount of time the camera's shutter stays open to expose the sensor. Faster speeds freeze motion; slower speeds create motion blur.

White Balance – Adjusts the camera's color temperature to match the lighting conditions, ensuring accurate colors.

Resources & Recommended Gear List

(No Affiliate Links in Print)

To help you get the most out of your Canon EOS R6 Mark II, here are trusted tools and accessories used by working photographers and filmmakers:

- **Lenses** – Canon RF 50mm f/1.8 STM (portraits), Canon RF 24–70mm f/2.8L IS USM (versatile workhorse), Canon RF 70–200mm f/2.8L IS USM (sports and wildlife).

- **Memory Cards** – V90-rated SD cards for high-bitrate 4K recording.

- **Tripods & Monopods** – Manfrotto Befree Advanced (travel), Benro A48T Monopod (sports/event shooting).

- **Microphones** – Rode VideoMic NTG (directional shotgun), Sennheiser XSW-D Lavalier Set (interviews).

- **Lighting** – Aputure Amaran 100d LED light with softbox for controlled, flattering light.

- **Cleaning Tools** – Giottos Rocket Blower, lens cleaning pen, microfiber cloths.

- **Camera Protection** – Rain covers for outdoor shoots, padded camera bags from Think Tank or Lowepro.

- **Editing Software** – Adobe Lightroom (photos), Adobe Premiere Pro (video), DaVinci Resolve (free, powerful color grading).

Index *(Organized by Shooting Scenario and Feature)*

Acknowledgments

Photography is not just about cameras and lenses — it's about the people who inspire us to see the world differently.

I am grateful to the photographers, filmmakers, and mentors who shared their wisdom, challenged my eye, and encouraged me to dig deeper into both the technical and creative sides of this craft.

To my fellow Canon shooters in the field, the wedding videographers who work tirelessly under pressure, the travel bloggers who shoot until the light is gone, and the YouTube educators who give freely of their knowledge — thank you. Your work, your mistakes, and your victories have shaped this guide.

Finally, to every reader who picks up this book: you are the reason it exists. The questions you ask, the struggles you share, and the progress you make inspire me to keep writing and refining resources like this one.

About The Author

Randy Osborn is a trusted name in the world of camera education, known for transforming complex gear manuals into simple, step-by-step guides that anyone can understand. With over a decade of experience working hands-on with leading camera systems—from Sony and Canon to Nikon, Leica, and more—Randy has helped thousands of photographers, content creators, and everyday users get the most out of their cameras without the overwhelm.

Driven by a passion for accessible learning, Randy creates user-friendly books that strip away the jargon and focus on real-world usage. Whether you're shooting your first vlog, learning manual mode for the first time, or simply trying to take better family photos, Randy's guides are designed to make every setting click.

Each book combines clear instruction, practical tips, and

relatable language, making it easy for beginners and seasoned hobbyists alike to master their gear and capture life with confidence.

When he's not writing, Randy enjoys field testing new camera releases, hosting beginner-friendly workshops, and exploring hidden photography gems across the globe.

Join the journey to sharper skills and smarter shooting—one page at a time.